Scott Foresman
Reading

Imagine That!

Imagine That!

Finding My Place

The Whole Wide World

Getting the Job Done

Scott Foresman

About the Cover Artist
As a child, Daniel Craig was crazy about dinosaurs, but in his Minneapolis home, his only pets are his cats, Isaac and Noah, and Winston, a dog. His pets often appear in his paintings.

ISBN 0-673-62161-8

Copyright © 2000 Addison-Wesley Educational Publishers Inc.

5 6 7 8 9 10-VH-06 05 04 03 02 01 00

Scott Foresman Reading

Imagine That!

Program Authors

Peter Afflerbach

James Beers

Camille Blachowicz

Candy Dawson Boyd

Deborah Diffily

Dolores Gaunty-Porter

Violet Harris

Donald Leu

Susan McClanahan

Dianne Monson

Bertha Pérez

Sam Sebesta

Karen Kring Wixson

Scott Foresman

Editorial Offices: Glenview, Illinois • New York, New York
Sales Offices: Reading, Massachusetts • Duluth, Georgia • Glenview, Illinois
Carrollton, Texas • Menlo Park, California

Contents

Finding My Place

Celebrity Author
Janet Stevens

Unit 1

Contents

THE WHOLE WIDE
WORLD

Unit 2

Contents

Getting the Job Done

Unit 3

9

janet steven

Dear Reader,

When I was growing up, I lived in many places because my dad was in the Navy. In third grade, I was the new kid . . . again.

My older brother and sister were straight A students. I was just okay at school. Good grades did not come easily for me. My older brother and sister were very smart. School seemed easy for them. I wanted to be smart. I thought I was not.

In third grade our class was divided into reading groups. The groups all had names: Cardinals, Robins, and Blue Jays. Cardinals were the best readers, the fastest readers.

We took a reading test to find out which bird we would be. I tried to read fast so I would be a Cardinal. But the story didn't make much sense to me when I read it that fast. "TIME'S UP!" said Mrs. Munsen.

Sometimes it's tough being the new kid. I felt as if I needed to impress everyone so they would like me. I needed to be a Cardinal. My stomach ached; my palms sweated. I thought, "Cardinals. Please make me a

Cardinal!" Then Mrs. Munsen called out the groups. She read the names of the Cardinal Reading Group. And she didn't call me.

Back in third grade, I never really understood that reading could be fun. Then one day something happened. I checked out *The Yearling* from the library. I brought it home and read it slowly, by myself. I reread parts I didn't understand; I looked up words I didn't know or asked my mom what they meant. I found a book that touched my heart. I laughed, and cried, and felt that I was reading for the first time.

It no longer mattered that I was only a Blue Jay. What was important was that I was reading and liking it. And you know what happened? Reading became easier. The more I read, the better a reader I became. It's just like basketball. You have to practice jump shots.

Wouldn't it be fun to show Mrs. Munsen all the books I've written and illustrated as an adult! I know now that being a Cardinal is not so very important. After all, I'm a Blue Jay who can write and illustrate books!

Finding My Place

How do friends and family help us grow?

Skill Lesson

Sequence

- **Sequence** is the order things happen in a story.

- Clue words, such as *before* and *after*, can tell you when something happens.

- Dates and times of day can also tell you when something happens.

- Picture in your mind what is happening. If the order does not make sense, try to figure out an order that does make sense.

Read "First Day at Camp" from *Arnie Goes to Camp* by Nancy Carlson.

Talk About It

1. When Arnie misses Louanne, what happens next that makes him not miss her so much?

2. When does Stretch take the campers on a hike? What clue words help you know this?

First Day at Camp

by Nancy Carlson

Arnie, who doesn't want to go to camp, has arrived with other campers for the first day.

When they arrived at camp, Arnie met his counselor Stretch. Stretch was eighteen years old and wore all sorts of camping gear on his belt. "Stretch is kind of neat," Arnie thought.

When they all hiked to their cabin, Arnie thought of his mom. He felt like crying.

Arnie's bunk-mate was a kid named Ted. Ted liked to play tricks. Arnie thought of his friend, Louanne. He missed her.

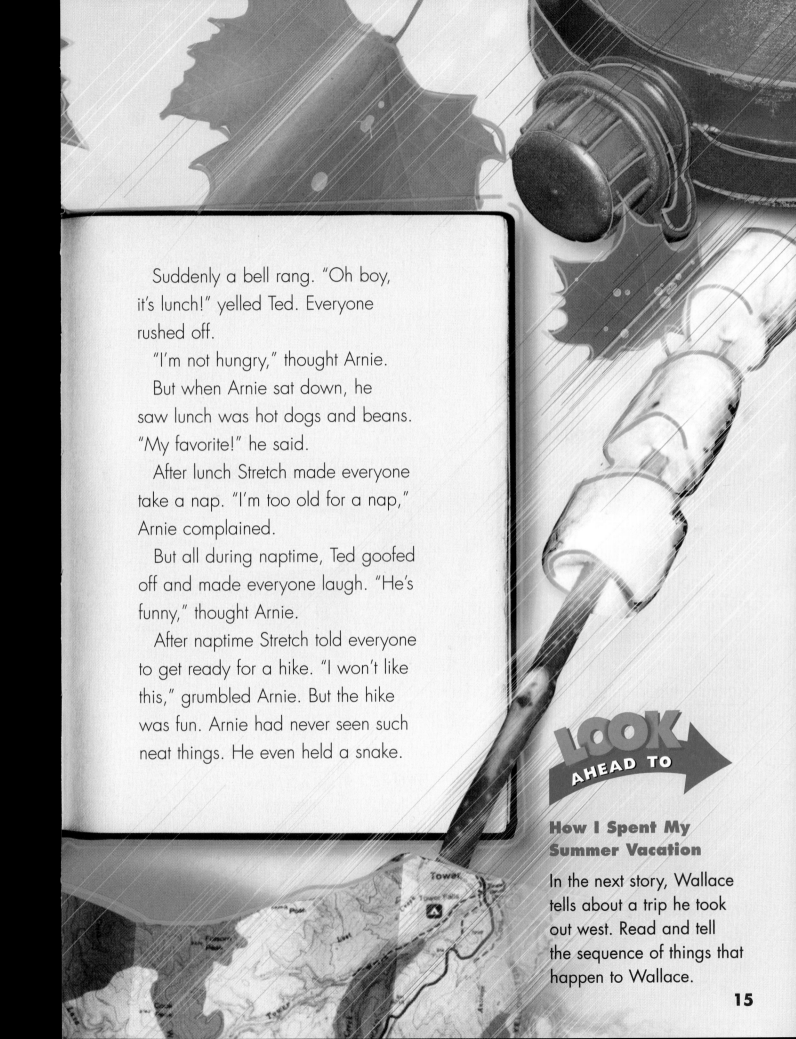

Suddenly a bell rang. "Oh boy, it's lunch!" yelled Ted. Everyone rushed off.

"I'm not hungry," thought Arnie.

But when Arnie sat down, he saw lunch was hot dogs and beans. "My favorite!" he said.

After lunch Stretch made everyone take a nap. "I'm too old for a nap," Arnie complained.

But all during naptime, Ted goofed off and made everyone laugh. "He's funny," thought Arnie.

After naptime Stretch told everyone to get ready for a hike. "I won't like this," grumbled Arnie. But the hike was fun. Arnie had never seen such neat things. He even held a snake.

LOOK AHEAD TO

How I Spent My Summer Vacation

In the next story, Wallace tells about a trip he took out west. Read and tell the sequence of things that happen to Wallace.

15

Words to Know

cowboys imagination summer
vacation visit west

When you read, you may come across a word you don't know. To figure out the meaning of the unfamiliar word, look for clues in the words around it. A clue can be in a description near the unknown word.

Read this paragraph. Notice how the description of *cowboys* helps you understand what it means.

A Trip to the Ranch

In my imagination, cowboys cook over fires after the long days of riding horses. Last summer when school was out, I went on vacation. On a visit to my uncle's ranch, I saw cowboys herd cattle, find a lost calf, and fix a fence. As the sun sank in the west, the cowboys did cook over the fire. But I felt lucky—I saw what their job is really like!

Talk About It

Tell a friend what you would like to do at a ranch. Use vocabulary words.

16

How I Spent My Summer Vacation

Written and
Illustrated by
Mark Teague

When summer began, I headed out west.
My parents had told me I needed a rest.
"Your imagination," they said, "is getting too wild.
It will do you some good to relax for a while."

So they put me aboard a westbound train
To visit Aunt Fern in her house on the plains.

But I was captured by cowboys,
A wild-looking crowd.
Their manners were rough
and their voices were loud.

"I'm trying to get to my aunt's house," I said.
But they carried me off to their cow camp instead.

The Cattle Boss growled, as he told me to sit,
"We need a new cowboy. Our old cowboy quit.
We could sure use your help. So what do you say?"
I thought for a minute, then I told him, "Okay."

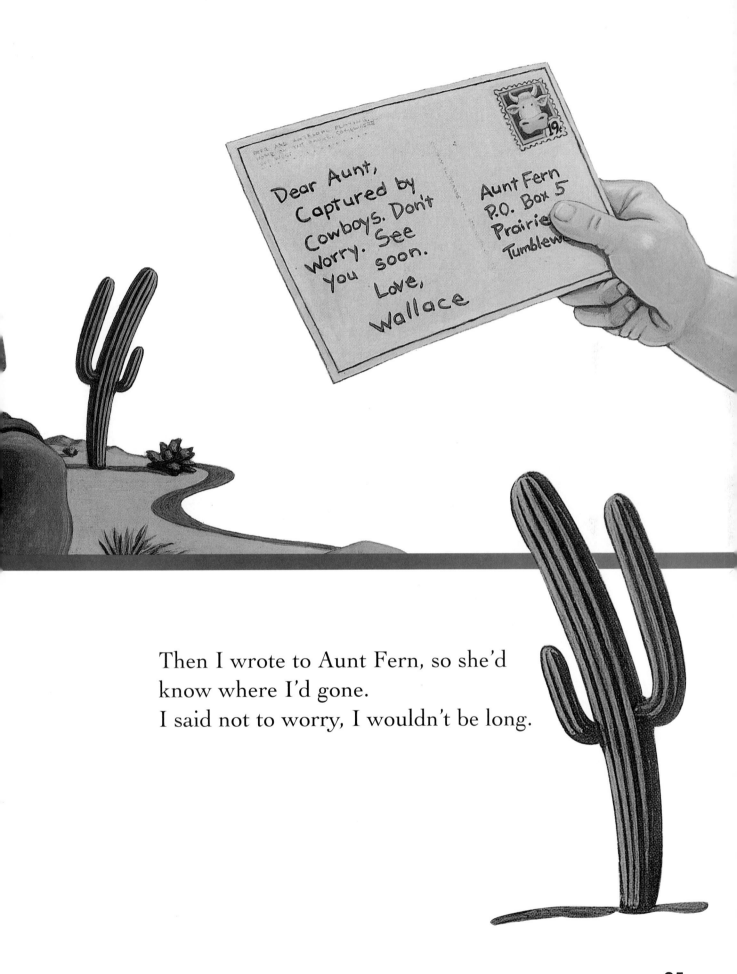

Then I wrote to Aunt Fern, so she'd
know where I'd gone.
I said not to worry, I wouldn't be long.

That night I was given a new set of clothes.
Soon I looked like a wrangler from my head to my toes.
But there's more to a cowboy than boots and a hat,
I found out the next day
And the day after that.

Each day I discovered some new cowboy tricks.
From roping
And riding
To making fire with sticks.
Slowly the word spread
all over the land:
"That wrangler 'Kid Bleff'
is a first-rate cowhand!"

The day finally came
when the roundup was through.
Aunt Fern called: "Come on over.
Bring your cowboys with you."
She was cooking a barbecue
that very same day.
So we cleaned up (a little)
and we headed her way.

The food was delicious. There was plenty to eat.
And the band that was playing just couldn't be beat.

But suddenly I noticed a terrible sight.
The cattle were stirring and stamping with fright.
It's a scene I'll remember till my very last day.
"They're gonna stampede!" I heard somebody say.
Just then they came charging. They charged right at *me!*
I looked for a hiding place—
a rock, or a tree.

33

What I found was a tablecloth spread out on the ground.
So I turned like a matador
And spun it around.
It was a new kind of cowboying, a fantastic display!
The cattle were frightened and stampeded . . . away!

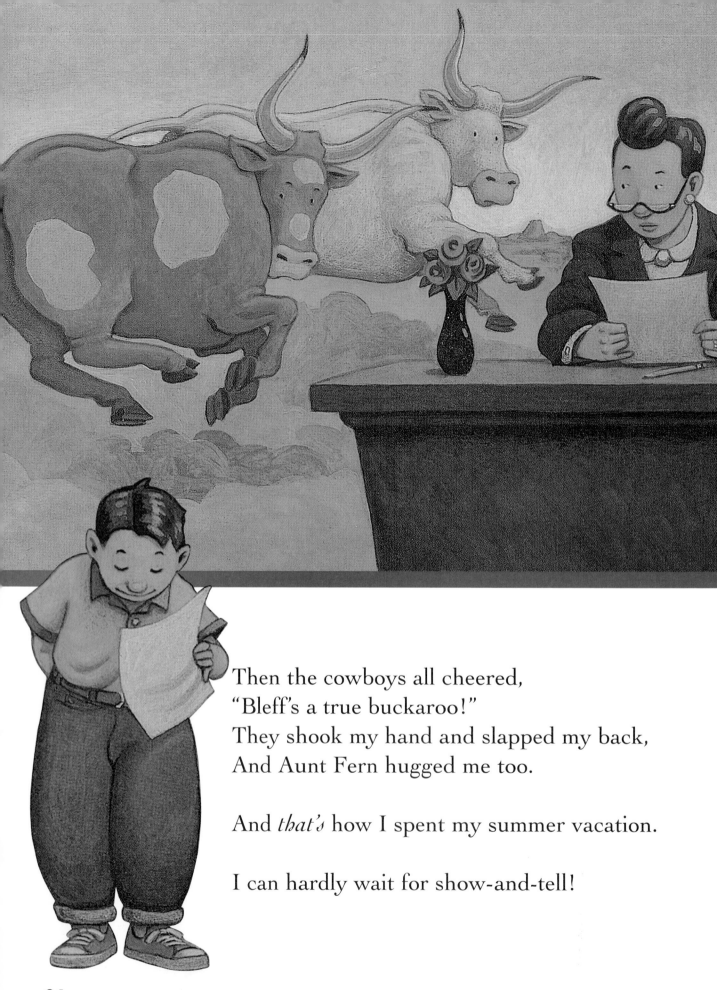

Then the cowboys all cheered,
"Bleff's a true buckaroo!"
They shook my hand and slapped my back,
And Aunt Fern hugged me too.

And *that's* how I spent my summer vacation.

I can hardly wait for show-and-tell!

Mark Teague

When Mark Teague was a child, he loved picture books. He especially loved writing and illustrating his own picture books. As a young man, Mr. Teague worked in a bookstore. While looking at the picture books in the store, he remembered how much fun he had when he made up his own stories. He decided to write more stories—and get them published this time.

Now Mr. Teague's stories and pictures are in books that are read by thousands of people. One thing has not changed about the way he makes his books, though. "I use a pencil for drawing and a huge eraser for erasing until I get it right," Mr. Teague says.

Other stories by Mark Teague that you might enjoy include *The Trouble with the Johnsons* and *Moog-Moog, Space Barber.*

Reader Response

Open for Discussion

Imagine going on your own Wild West adventure. What would happen on your adventure?

Comprehension Check

1. Do you think any part of Wallace's Wild West story could be true? Why or why not?

2. The cowboys call Wallace a "true buckaroo." What words from the story explain what the cowboys mean?

3. Wallace says he can hardly wait for show-and-tell. What do you think he means?

4. Clue words such as *first, next, last* or the time of day tell the **sequence,** or order, of events. List clue words in the story that tell when things happen.

5. Tell the **sequence** of events that happened to Wallace.

Round-Robin Story

Make up a round-robin story with three or four classmates. Begin the story, which can be real or imaginary, with "Last summer I took a trip to . . .."
For five minutes take turns adding sentences. When the time is up, record your story. Discuss how realistic or fantastic your story is.

PECOS BILL

retold by Ariane Dewey

Pecos Bill is a tall-tale cowboy hero of the Old West. Bill could rope anything, even a streak of lightning. The tales say he was raised in the wilds of Texas by coyotes. Here's what happened on the day Bill met a cowboy named Curly Joe.

"My name is Curly Joe. What's yours?" said the cowboy.

"Bill," said Bill.

They were standing by the Pecos River. "Pecos Bill sounds better," said the cowboy.

And that's how Pecos Bill got his name.

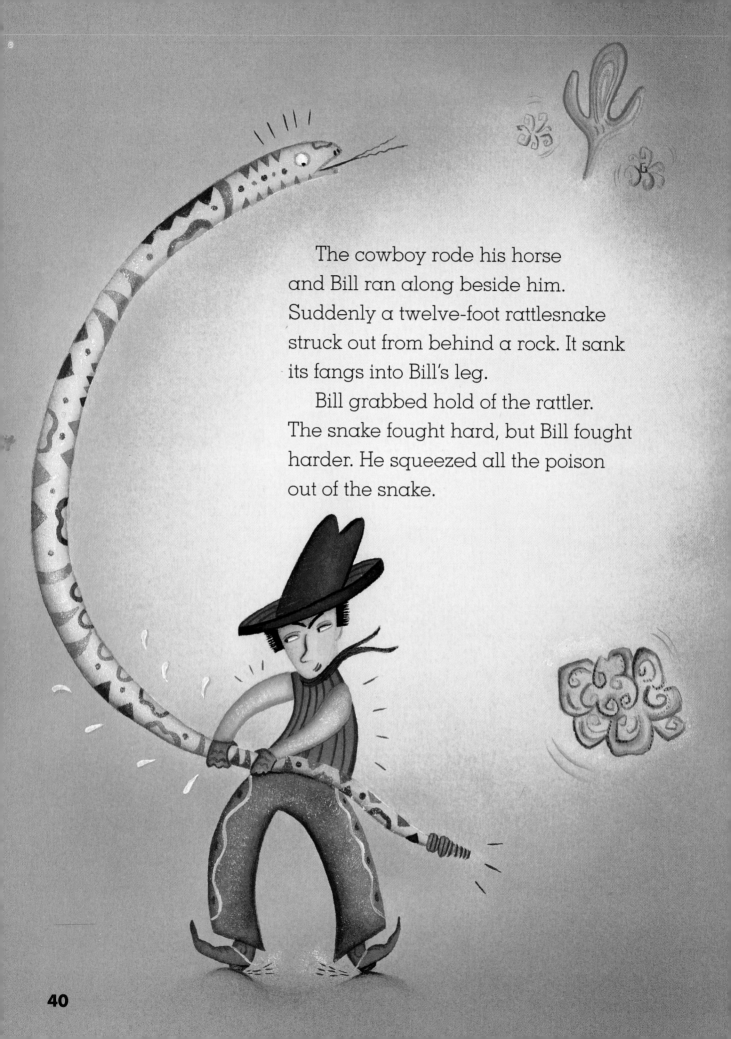

The cowboy rode his horse
and Bill ran along beside him.
Suddenly a twelve-foot rattlesnake
struck out from behind a rock. It sank
its fangs into Bill's leg.

Bill grabbed hold of the rattler.
The snake fought hard, but Bill fought
harder. He squeezed all the poison
out of the snake.

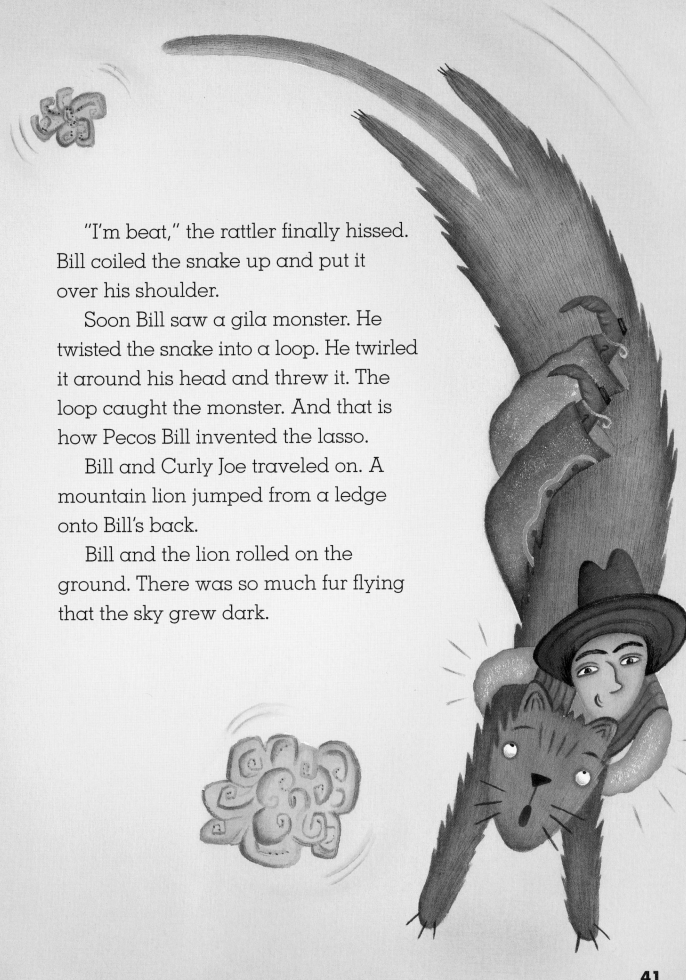

"I'm beat," the rattler finally hissed. Bill coiled the snake up and put it over his shoulder.

Soon Bill saw a gila monster. He twisted the snake into a loop. He twirled it around his head and threw it. The loop caught the monster. And that is how Pecos Bill invented the lasso.

Bill and Curly Joe traveled on. A mountain lion jumped from a ledge onto Bill's back.

Bill and the lion rolled on the ground. There was so much fur flying that the sky grew dark.

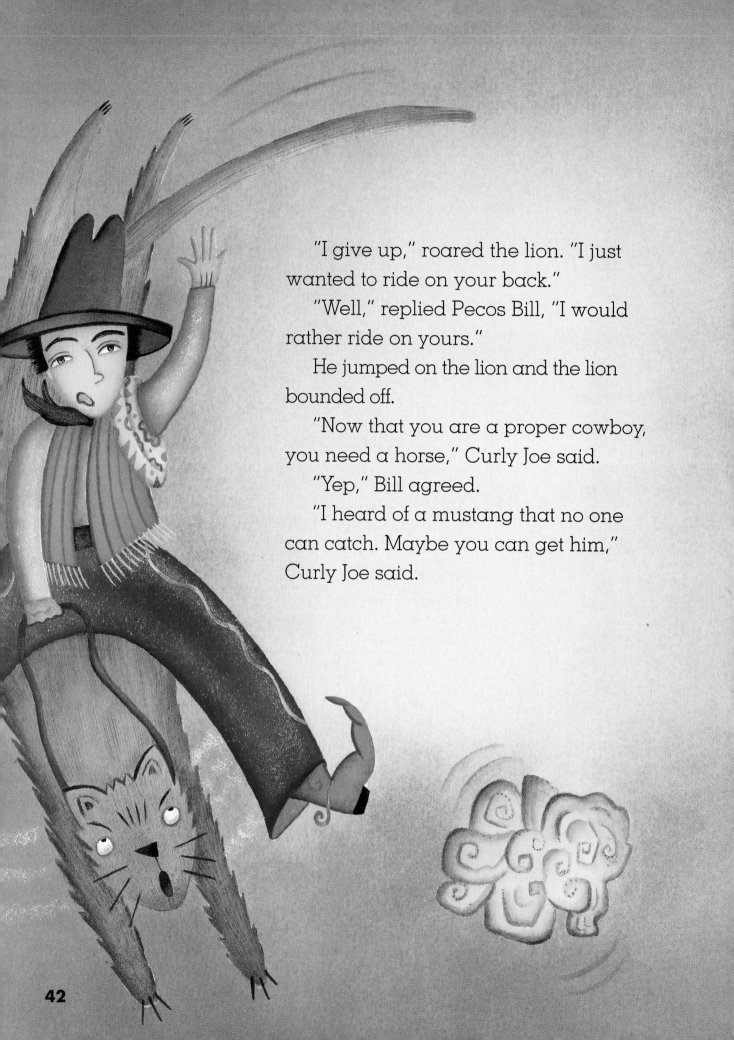

"I give up," roared the lion. "I just wanted to ride on your back."

"Well," replied Pecos Bill, "I would rather ride on yours."

He jumped on the lion and the lion bounded off.

"Now that you are a proper cowboy, you need a horse," Curly Joe said.

"Yep," Bill agreed.

"I heard of a mustang that no one can catch. Maybe you can get him," Curly Joe said.

Bill started off at once. He could run a hundred miles an hour. He tracked that mustang from Texas to Montana and back.

In Colorado, the mustang stopped for a drink.

Bill said, "You're the fastest horse that ever was and I'm the greatest cowboy. Let's team up."

And they did.

Drawing Conclusions

- A **conclusion** is a decision you make about what happens in a story.

- Authors give details about what happens. They may give clues about why things happen.

- You **draw conclusions** when you use what you know to make decisions that make sense about characters or events.

Read "Spider's Story" from *Three up a Tree* by James Marshall.

Write About It

1. After reading, write the word *chicken* at the top of a sheet of paper. Write two sentences about how the chicken feels and how you know this.

2. Share your conclusions with your classmates.

Spider's Story

by James Marshall

A chicken caught the wrong bus. She found herself in a bad part of town—the part where foxes live. "Uh-oh," she said.

Quickly she pulled down her hat and waited for the next bus.

But very soon—you guessed it— a hungry fox came along and sat beside her.

LOOK
AHEAD TO

Goldilocks and the Three Bears

In the next story, Goldilocks does just what she was not supposed to do. Read and get ready to draw your own conclusions about the characters.

Words to Know

breakfast	forest	promise
comfortable	gobbled	
cozy	hungry	

Words that have similar meanings, like *hat* and *cap,* are **synonyms**. To find the meaning of a word, look for clues in words nearby. Sometimes the clue is a synonym.

Read the story. Notice how *snug* and *warm* help you understand *cozy*.

The Three Little Bears

Deep in the <u>forest</u>, three bear cubs were <u>cozy</u> in their bed, feeling snug, warm, and <u>comfortable</u>. But they wouldn't go to sleep. So Mother Bear told them a story: "Once upon a time, three bears missed their <u>breakfast</u> because they stayed up too late the night before. A little girl came into their house. She was so <u>hungry</u> that she <u>gobbled</u> up their breakfast."
The cubs said, "We <u>promise</u> to go to sleep."

Talk About It

Use vocabulary words to tell a friend your favorite tale.

Once there was a little girl called Goldilocks.

"What a sweet child," said someone new in town.

"That's what *you* think," said a neighbor.

One morning Goldilocks's mother sent her to buy muffins in the next village. "You must promise *not* to take the shortcut through the forest," she said. "I've heard that bears live there."

"I promise," said Goldilocks. But to tell the truth Goldilocks was one of those naughty little girls who do *exactly* as they please.

Meanwhile in a clearing deeper inside the forest, in a charming house all their own, a family of brown bears was sitting down to breakfast.

"Patooie!" cried big old Papa Bear. "This porridge is scalding! I've burned my tongue!"

"I'm dying!" cried Baby Bear.

"Now really," said Mama Bear, who was of medium size. "That's quite enough."

"I know," said Papa Bear. "Why don't we go for a spin while the porridge is cooling?"

"Excellent," said Mama Bear. So they got on their rusty old bicycle and off they went.

A few minutes later Goldilocks arrived at the bears' house. She walked right in without *even* bothering to knock. On the dining room table were three inviting bowls of porridge.

"I don't mind if I do," said Goldilocks, helping herself to the biggest bowl.

But the porridge in the biggest bowl was much too hot. "Patooie!" cried Goldilocks. And she spat it out.

Next she tasted the porridge in the medium-sized bowl. But that porridge was much too cold.

Then Goldilocks tasted the porridge in the little bowl, and it was *just right*—neither too hot nor too cold. In fact she liked it so much that she gobbled it all up.

Feeling full and satisfied Goldilocks thought it would be great fun to have a look around. Right away she noticed a lot of coarse brown fur everywhere. "They must have kitties," she said.

In the parlor there were three chairs. "I don't mind if I do," she said, climbing into the biggest one. But the biggest chair was much too hard, and she just couldn't get comfortable.

Next she sat in the medium-sized chair. But that chair was much too soft. (And she thought she might *never* get out of it.)

Then Goldilocks sat in the little chair, and that was *just right*—neither too hard nor too soft. In fact she liked it so much that she rocked and rocked—until the chair fell completely to pieces!

Now, all that rocking left Goldilocks quite
tuckered out. "I could take a little snooze," she
said. So she went to look for a comfy place to nap.
Upstairs were three beds. "I don't mind if I do,"
said Goldilocks. And she got into the biggest one.
But the head of the biggest bed was much too high.

Next she tried the medium-sized bed. But the
head of that bed was much too low. Then Goldilocks
tried the little bed, and it was *just right*. Soon she
was all nice and cozy and sound asleep. She did not
hear the bears come home.

The three bears were mighty hungry. But when they went in for breakfast, they could scarcely believe their eyes!

"Somebody has been in my porridge!" said Papa Bear.

"Somebody has been in *my* porridge!" said Mama Bear.

"Somebody has been in my porridge," said Baby Bear. "And eaten it all up!"

In the parlor the three bears were in for another little surprise.

"Somebody has been sitting in my chair!" said Papa Bear.

"Somebody has been sitting in *my* chair," said Mama Bear.

"Somebody has been sitting in my chair," said Baby Bear. "And broken it to smithereens!"

The three bears went upstairs on tiptoe (not knowing what they would discover). At first everything seemed fine. But then Papa Bear lay down on his big brass bed.

"Somebody has been lying in my bed!" he cried. And he was not amused.

"Egads!" cried Mama Bear. "Somebody has been lying in *my* bed!"

"Look!" cried Baby Bear. "Somebody has been lying in my bed. And she's still there!"

"Now see here!" roared Papa Bear. Goldilocks woke up with a start. And her eyes nearly popped out of her head. But before the bears could demand a proper explanation, Goldilocks was out of bed, out the window, and on her way home.

"Who *was* that little girl?" asked Baby Bear.

"I have no idea," said Mama Bear. "But I hope we never see her again."

And they never did.

About the Author/Illustrator

James Marshall

James Marshall was a teacher who had a hobby. He liked to draw. One day a friend saw his drawings and convinced him to see a publisher of children's books. Mr. Marshall met with the person and the next day was asked to illustrate a book. Later he started writing stories to go along with the pictures he drew.

One time Mr. Marshall had a dream that a character in one of his books was upset with him. "She had become very cross with me. She wanted better stories, better lines!" The character told Mr. Marshall that if she didn't get them she was going to another illustrator's house!

Mr. Marshall's retelling of *Goldilocks and the Three Bears* was a Caldecott Honor Book in 1989. He also has retold the stories *Little Red Riding Hood* and *Cinderella*.

Reader Response

Open for Discussion

Some people believe folk tales teach important lessons. What lesson can you learn from this story? Explain.

Comprehension Check

1. A new person in town says Goldilocks is a sweet child. A neighbor replies, "That's what *you* think." What does the neighbor mean? Find examples from the story to explain.

2. The pictures in *Goldilocks and the Three Bears* help tell the story. Find your favorite picture. Explain how it helps tell the story.

3. What do you think would have happened if Goldilocks hadn't jumped out the window? Explain.

4. Actions can help you **draw conclusions** about someone. What kind of girl is Goldilocks? Give examples of actions from the story.

5. Now **draw conclusions** about Mama Bear. What is she like? How do you know?

Pantomime

Pantomime is a way of acting without speaking. Choose a classmate for each character in the story. Have two or three other classmates take turns reading all or part of the story while the mimes (the silent actors) show the action.

Author's Purpose

- **Author's purpose** is the author's reason for writing.

- An author may try to inform, or explain something.

- An author may try to entertain you or let you have fun with the reading.

Read "A Cowboy's Rope" from *The Cowboy's Handbook* by Tod Cody.

Talk About It

1. What is the author's purpose for writing this? Why do you think so?

2. What things about a cowboy's rope did the author tell you that you did not know?

A Cowboy's Rope

by Tod Cody

The braided rawhide leather rope the *vaquero* used was called *la reata*, and this was changed by the cowboy into "lariat." The lariat's main use was for lassoing, but it was also used to drag firewood, to haul out wagons stuck in the mud, and to build makeshift corrals.

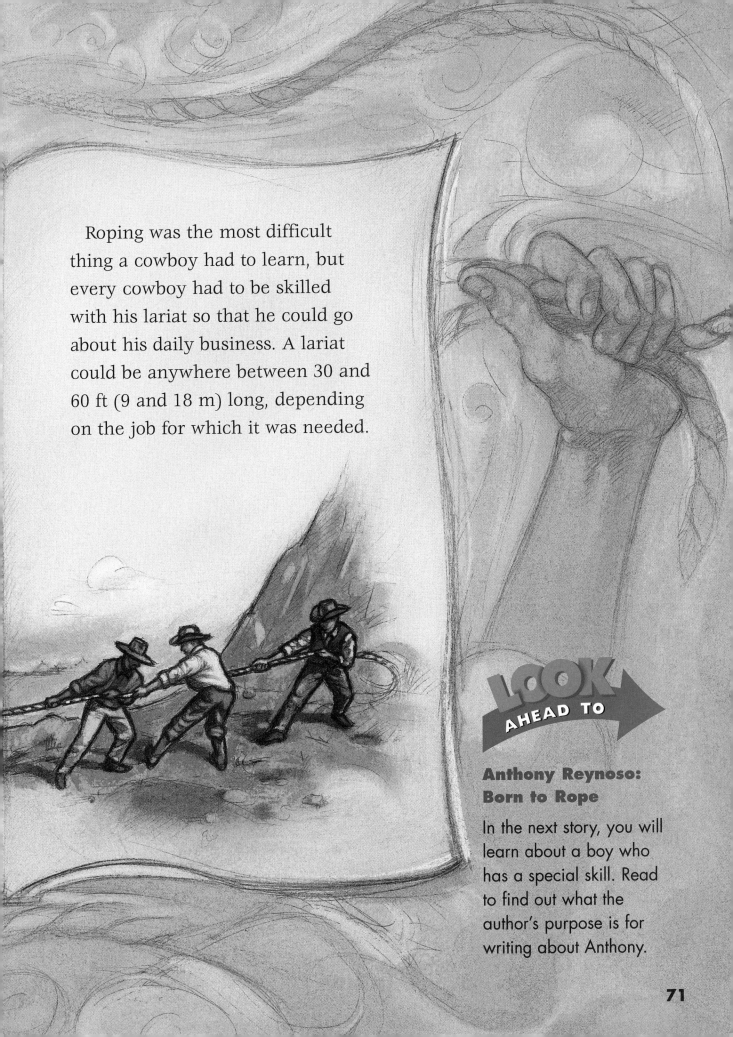

Roping was the most difficult thing a cowboy had to learn, but every cowboy had to be skilled with his lariat so that he could go about his daily business. A lariat could be anywhere between 30 and 60 ft (9 and 18 m) long, depending on the job for which it was needed.

LOOK AHEAD TO

Anthony Reynoso: Born to Rope

In the next story, you will learn about a boy who has a special skill. Read to find out what the author's purpose is for writing about Anthony.

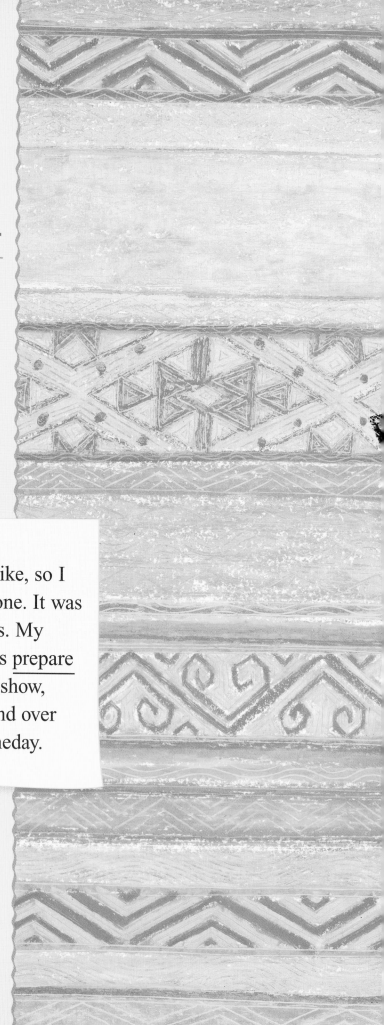

Words to Know

favorite   practice   tourists
rodeo   prepare   grandfather

When you read, you may come across words you don't know. Look for clues in the words or sentences near the word to figure out what it means.

Read this paragraph. Figure out the meaning of *practice* by reading the words around it.

Ride 'Em Cowboy!

I was curious about what a <u>rodeo</u> is like, so I asked my <u>grandfather</u> to take me to one. It was fun being <u>tourists</u> with other travelers. My <u>favorite</u> part was watching the clowns <u>prepare</u> and <u>practice</u> for their act. Before the show, they do funny and hard stunts over and over again. I hope I can be in a rodeo someday.

Write About It

Where would you like to travel? Write a postcard from your trip. Use some of the vocabulary words.

ANTHONY REYNOSO
Born to Rope

BY MARTHA COOPER AND GINGER GORDON

My name is Anthony Reynoso. I'm named after my father, who is holding the white horse, and my grandfather, who is holding the dappled horse. We all rope and ride Mexican Rodeo style on my grandfather's ranch outside of Phoenix, Arizona.

As soon as I could stand, my dad gave me a rope. I had my own little hat and everything else I needed to dress as a *charro*. That's what a Mexican cowboy is called.

It's a good thing I started when I was little, because it takes years to learn to rope.

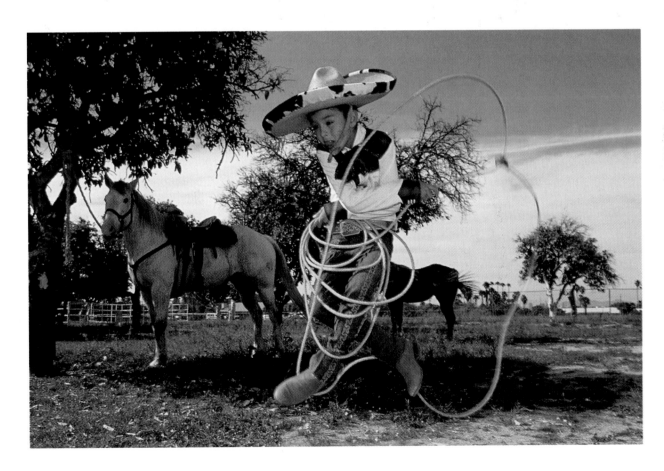

I live with my mom and dad in the little Mexican American and Yaqui Indian town of Guadalupe. All my grandparents live close by. This will help a lot when the new baby comes. My mom is pregnant.

I've got a secret about Guadalupe. I know where there are petroglyphs in the rocks right near my house. My favorite looks like a man with a shield. People carved these petroglyphs hundreds of years ago. Why did they do it? I wonder what the carvings mean.

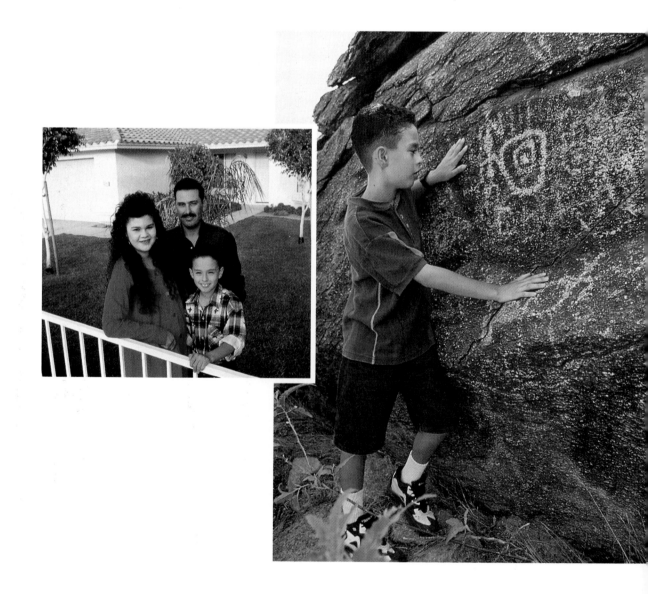

Every Sunday morning the old Mexican Mission church is packed. At Easter, lots of people come to watch the Yaqui Indian ceremonies in the center of town. No one's allowed to take photographs, but an artist painted a wall showing the Yaqui dancers.

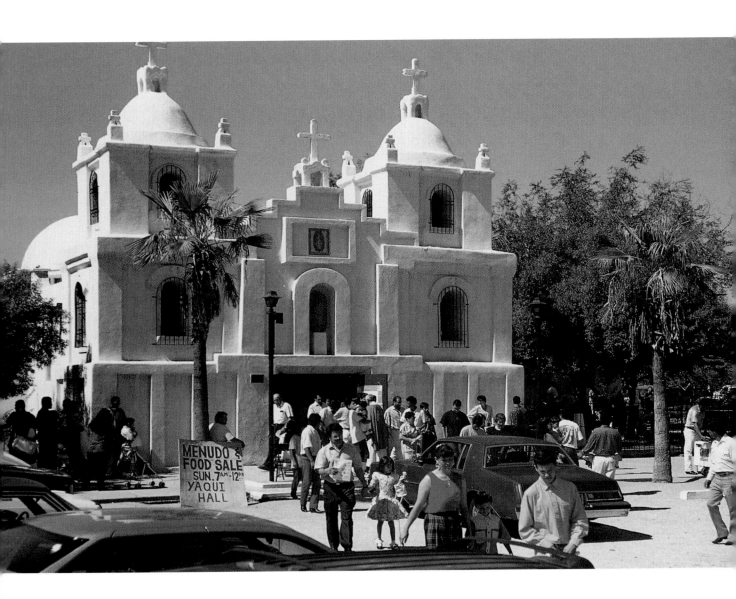

Some Sundays, we go to Casa Reynoso, my grandparents' restaurant. If it's very busy, my cousins and I pitch in. When there's time, my grandmother lets me help in the kitchen. Casa Reynoso has the best Mexican food in town.

On holidays, we go to my grandfather's ranch. Once a year, we all get dressed up for a family photo.

I've got lots of cousins. Whenever there's a birthday we have a piñata. We smash it with a stick until all the candy falls out. Then we scramble to grab as much as we can hold.

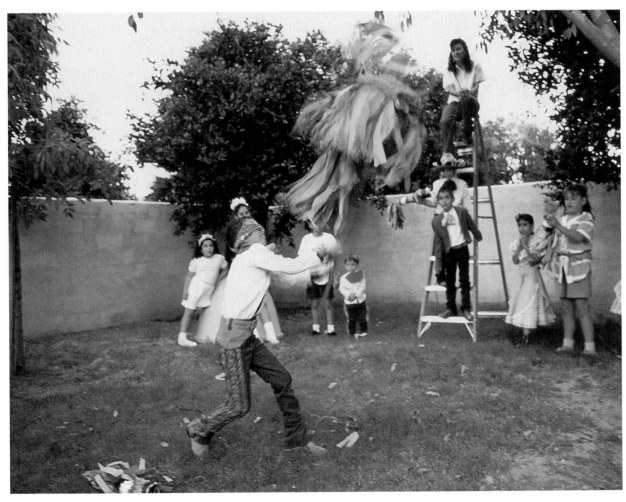

Best of all, at the ranch we get to practice roping on horseback. My dad's always trying something new . . . and so am I!

In Mexico, the Rodeo is the national sport. The most famous charros there are like sports stars here.

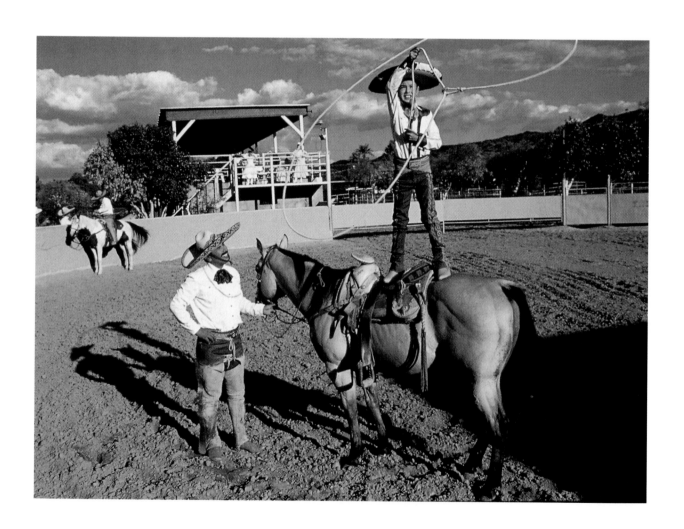

On weekdays, Dad runs his landscape business, Mom works in a public school, and I go to school. I wait for the bus with other kids at the corner of my block.

I always come to school with my homework done. When I'm in class, I forget about roping and riding. I don't think anyone in school knows about it except my best friends.

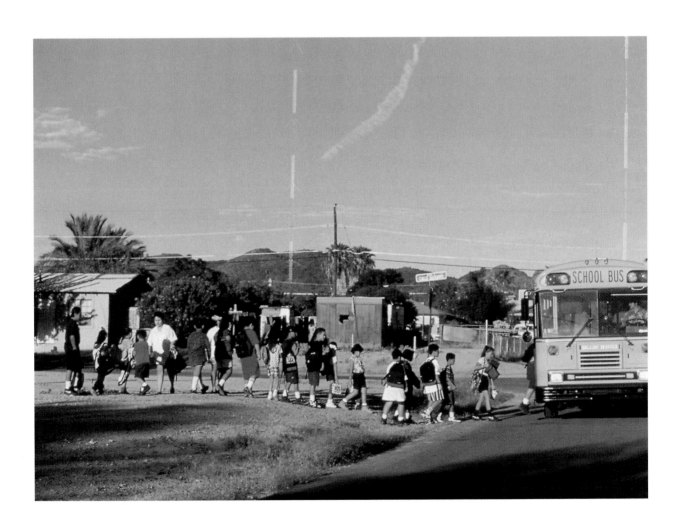

It's different when I get home. I practice hard with Dad. He's a good teacher and shows me everything his father taught him. We spend a lot of time practicing for shows at schools, malls, and rodeos. We are experts at passing the rope. Our next big exhibition is in Sedona, about two hours away by car.

After rope practice we shoot a few baskets. Dad's pretty good at that too!

On Friday after school, Dad and I prepare our ropes for the show in Sedona. They've got to be just right.

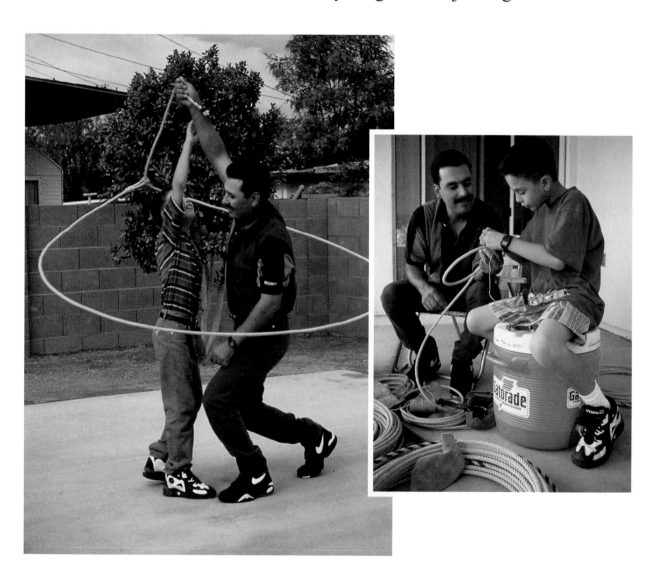

Everything's ready for tomorrow, so I can take a break and go through my basketball cards. I decide which ones I want to buy, sell, and trade. Collecting basketball cards is one of my favorite hobbies.

It's Saturday! Time for the show in Sedona. I get a little nervous watching the other performers. I sure wouldn't want to get messed up in my own rope in front of all these people!

After the Mexican hat dance, we're next!

My dad goes first . . .

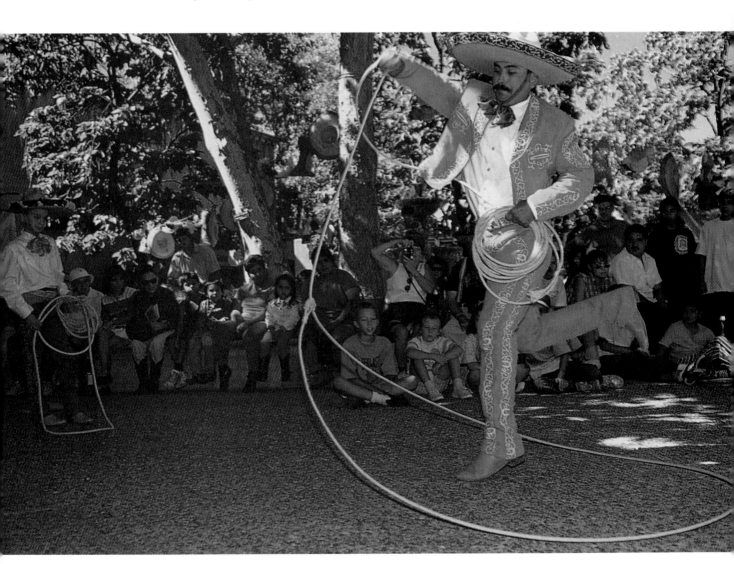

and then it's my turn. While the mariachis play, I do my stuff.

Even Dad can't spin the rope from his teeth like this!

Then Dad and I rope together, just like we practiced. It's hard to do with our wide charro hats on. When my dad passes the rope to me and I spin it well, he says he has passed the Mexican Rodeo tradition on to me. Now it's up to me to keep it going.

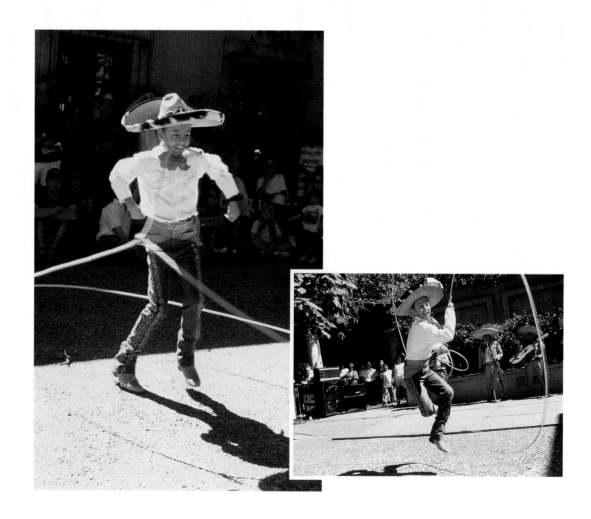

Mom is our best fan. She always comes with us. It makes me feel good to know she's out there watching.

Sometimes tourists want us to pose for pictures with them. It makes me feel like a celebrity.

After the show, boy, are we hungry! We pack up and eat a quick lunch. Then we go to a special place called Slide Rock.

Slide Rock is a natural water slide where kids have played for hundreds, maybe even thousands, of years. It's cold today! I'd rather come back in the summer when it's hot. But Dad pulls me in anyway. Brrr!

Time to go home. Next time we come to Sedona, the baby will be with us. I wonder if it will be a boy or a girl. It's hard to wait!

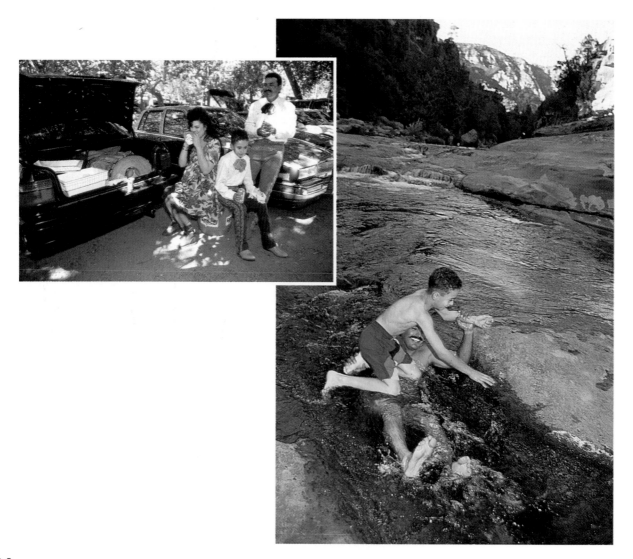

I'm going to love being a big brother. Pretty soon the baby will be wearing my old boots and learning how to rope from me.

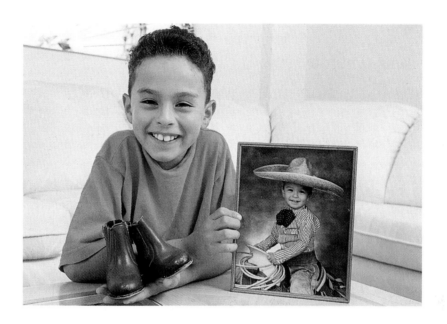

About the Author and the Photographer

GINGER GORDON
MARTHA COOPER

Anthony Reynoso: Born to Rope is a true story told in photographs about a Mexican American boy.

Ginger Gordon, a teacher in New York City, wrote the words to go along with the pictures. She says she gets her ideas from her students.

Martha Cooper took the pictures of Anthony Reynoso and his family. She has taken pictures for other books and magazines too.

Open for Discussion

Roping takes a lot of practice. Do you think everyone could learn to rope? Why or why not?

Comprehension Check

1. Do you think Anthony enjoys roping? What parts of the story make you think as you do?

2. Anthony does other things besides roping. Name them.

3. In *How I Spent My Summer Vacation*, Wallace also learns to rope and do tricks. Who do you think would be better at roping and doing tricks, Anthony or Wallace? Why?

4. **Author's purpose** is the writer's reason for writing. Name one important purpose the author had for writing about Anthony. Why do you think so?

5. Often an **author** has more than one **purpose** for writing. Name another reason the author had for writing about Anthony. Why do you think so?

Hobby Book

Make a hobby book. First create an eye-catching cover. Then draw on each page, or use pictures from old magazines, to show a hobby you have or would like to have. Write two or three sentences under each picture telling why your hobby is special. Share your book with your classmates.

SPANISH PLACE-NAMES

by the Westridge Young Writers Workshop

COLORADO

Pueblo
(Small Town)

Trinidad
(Trinity)

ARIZONA

NEW MEXICO

OKLAHOMA

El Reno
(The Reindeer)

Caballo
(Horse)

Amarillo
(Yellow)

Agua Caliente
(Hot Water)

Casa Grande
(Big House)

Las Cruces
(The Crosses)

Ajo
(Garlic)

Dos Cabezas
(Two Heads)

TEXAS

San Antonio
(Saint Anthony)

El Paso
(The Pass)

Rio Grande
(Big River)

Reading Across Texts

Reading a Short Informational Article

✓ **Figure out the main idea.** Since the piece is short, you have to do that quickly.

✓ **Enjoy it!** Short pieces often tell interesting bits of information.

Focus Your Reading

This article tells how some places got Spanish names. As you read, think of the names of some places Anthony Reynoso might visit to perform his roping.

Have you ever wondered why so many places in the United States have Spanish names? It is estimated that over 100,000 Spaniards came west during the first half of the sixteenth century. When they came, they named many communities, rivers, areas, and settlements. Here are just a few for you to visit.

The next time you look at a map, try to see how many Spanish names you can find. A clue to look for is that many Spanish words end with a vowel. Spanish names for places often include: *san* (male saint), *santa* (female saint), *rio* (river), and the words *el, la, los,* or *las* (the).

Cause and Effect

- A **cause** is why something happens.

- An **effect** is what happens.

- Clue words can sometimes signal causes and effects.

- As you read, look for clue words, such as *if, then, because, since,* and *so,* to help you understand what happens and why it happens.

Read "Annabelle's Party" from *Herbie Jones* by Suzy Kline.

Write About It

1. Write the words *cause* and *effect* at the top of a sheet of paper. List some things that happen under *effect* and why they happen under *cause*.

2. Write down some clue words that signal what happens and why.

Annabelle's Party

by Suzy Kline

The phone rang, so Herbie picked it up. "Hello?"

"Double 030?"

Herbie cupped the phone and whispered, "Yeah . . . just a minute, 992." Herbie moved the phone and phone cord through the dining room and into the pantry off the kitchen. When he closed the door a rack of onions fell on him.

"What's that?" Raymond asked.

"Nothing, 992, just a bunch of onions."

"Huh?"

"Never mind. What's so important that we have to use code language?"

"You're getting an invitation to Annabelle Louisa Hodgekiss's birthday party."

Herbie sat down on two onions. "You've got to be kidding."

"Nope. I was at Mr. D's store and I heard Annabelle tell her mother that she needed nine invitations this year because she wanted to invite you to her birthday."

"Where were you?"

"Behind the magic markers. I wanted to find a purple one. Her mother was mad, too, because she had to buy another package of invitations. They only came eight to a package."

"Man, why do you suppose she wants ME to come?"

"Well, you're the spelling champ and all."

Herbie picked up the two onions he had been sitting on and started juggling them in the air. "I wish people would forget about that. Now I feel like I have to get a hundred every Friday—especially when Dad asks to see my spelling test as soon as I get home."

"That's deadly. Hey Herbie, I was thinkin', do you suppose Annabelle might use a few of those extra invitations?"

"Maybe."

"If she does, I bet she invites me too. She knows I'm your best friend."

LOOK AHEAD TO

Herbie and Annabelle

In the next story, you will read more about Herbie and Annabelle. Read and get ready to find out what happens and why.

Words to Know

coughs   pretend   discovered

secret   poems   sheet

curious

Many words have more than one meaning. To decide what a word means, look for clues in the words around it.

Read the list. Decide if *sheet* means "a piece of cloth" or "a single piece of paper."

Things to Do When Sick

When Joe <u>coughs</u> and stays in bed, he makes a list of things to do.

1. Find out who <u>discovered</u> the planets.
2. Write some silly <u>poems</u>.
3. <u>Pretend</u> to be famous and on TV.
4. Make up a <u>secret</u> code.
5. Read a book under the <u>sheet</u>.
6. Make up a story about a <u>curious</u> dog.

Write About It

Use vocabulary words to write a sick friend a get well card.

Herbie
and
Annabelle

by Suzy Kline

Who's Who

Herbie Jones likes to read but he has been in the lowest reading group for most of his life. He carries a notebook, writes poems, reads books about spiders, and enjoys teasing his older sister, Olivia. He hates doing skill sheets in his third-grade class at Laurel Woods Elementary School. Sometimes he uses his spy code number—Double 030—when he talks to his best friend, Raymond Martin, on the phone. Herbie cares what his parents think.

Annabelle Louisa Hodgekiss is the smartest girl in third grade. She is bossy and can be mean, but she works hard, is very neat, and always obeys the rules. When she's angry with Herbie, she gives him the silent treatment or puts red checks after his name in her notepad. She's a good athlete and tries to be first in every contest. Her initials, ALH, are on most of her things.

Mr. Hodgekiss is Annabelle's father. He likes making eggplant parmigiana, watching Annabelle play baseball, and cracking jokes. Annabelle doesn't think they're funny. Herbie does.

Narrator is like a stage manager. He or she establishes the setting, time, and character motivation. When necessary, this person moves the action.

SFX Person is the Sound Effects Person who makes special noises.

Characters: Narrator
SFX Person
Herbie Jones
Mr. Hodgekiss
Annabelle Louisa Hodgekiss

Setting: Annabelle's house

Time: After school

NARRATOR: Herbie rang Annabelle's doorbell.

SFX PERSON: Bzzzzzzz. Bzzzzzz.

HERBIE: I wish I didn't have to deliver these get well cards from the class. But the teacher said I *had* to because I live the closest. *(groans)*

NARRATOR: Mr. Hodgekiss answered the door.

MR. HODGEKISS: Hello, Herbie.

HERBIE: Hello, Mr. Hodgekiss. My teacher wanted me to drop these cards by for Annabelle. Would you please give them to her? *(waves good-bye)* Thanks, bye.

NARRATOR: Herbie turned around and headed down the steps.

MR. HODGEKISS: Just a minute, Herbie. Won't you come in and give the cards to Annabelle yourself? The doctor said she isn't contagious anymore.

HERBIE: *(to himself)* Whoa. I was supposed to deliver these cards to the door. Not go *in*. Miss Pinkham never said I had to do *that*.

MR. HODGEKISS: Just for a minute?

SFX PERSON: *(clears throat)*

HERBIE: Well . . . okay, Mr. Hodgekiss.

NARRATOR: Herbie felt his throat getting dry and raspy as he walked inside the house. When they got to Annabelle's door, they stopped.

MR. HODGEKISS: Before we go in, I must tell you something. Annabelle has been very stubborn about having the chicken pox.

SFX PERSON: *(clears throat again)*

HERBIE: *(answers like a squeaky frog)* Reaaaally?

NARRATOR: Herbie tried to act surprised but the fact was Herbie already knew Annabelle was stubborn—about everything.

MR. HODGEKISS: She insists on putting the sheet over her head every time someone comes in the room. She won't even let *me* see her face. Just her mother. She says when the spots and scabs are gone in a few days, she won't hide behind the sheet.

HERBIE: *(to Mr. Hodgekiss)* No kidding? Annabelle has a sheet over her head? *(to himself)* This is great! I didn't want to see her anyway.

MR. HODGEKISS: Maybe you'll have better luck. *(knocks on door)* May we come in, Annabelle?

ANNABELLE: Who's with you?

MR. HODGEKISS: Someone from school. He has some get well cards for you.

NARRATOR: Mr. Hodgekiss opened the door slowly. Herbie saw Annabelle sitting up in bed. The sheet was tucked behind her head.

ANNABELLE: Who is it?

MR. HODGEKISS: See for yourself, dear.

NARRATOR: Mr. Hodgekiss smiled as he walked out of the room. Herbie quickly looked around and sat down in a chair by Annabelle's desk.

SFX PERSON: *(coughs a few times and then clears throat)*

HERBIE: Hi . . . hi . . . Annabelle.

ANNABELLE: Do you have a cold, John, or is that your asthma acting up again?

HERBIE: *(to himself)* John? Hey, this could be fun. I'm visiting a ghost and now I can even pretend to be someone else. *(to Annabelle)* Just . . . just my asthma.

ANNABELLE: Did you bring me some cards?

HERBIE: Yup. Here's two.

ANNABELLE: Read them to me.

HERBIE: Sure. Here's one with a Viking ship on it.

ANNABELLE: I know that's from Raymond Martin. He always draws Viking ships.

HERBIE: Yup, and on the inside it says, "Bon Voyage."

ANNABELLE: BON VOYAGE? That's dumb. Bon Voyage means have a good trip. Having the chicken pox is NOT having fun, and you certainly can't go anywhere.

NARRATOR: Herbie remembered to cough a few times and act like John.

SFX PERSON: *(coughs, wheezes, and sneezes)*

HERBIE: Here's a real nice card. It has you in bed with your cat and a thermometer in your mouth.

ANNABELLE: Hmmmmm. I wonder who made that one?

HERBIE: It even has a poem inside. I'll read it.

Annabelle, Annabelle,
Sick in bed,
Spots on her nose
And spots on her head.
Think I will give her a
Bright red rose.
Then she knows
I will tickle her toes
With it.

ANNABELLE: *(giggles)* That's funny! Who wrote it?

NARRATOR: Herbie tipped back his chair.

HERBIE: Herbie Jones.

ANNABELLE: Herbie Jones wrote *that?*

HERBIE: The one and only.

NARRATOR: Annabelle was quiet for a moment.

ANNABELLE: Well, you know, John . . .

HERBIE: Yes, Annabelle . . .

ANNABELLE: I'm not speaking to Herbie . . .

HERBIE: Oh?

NARRATOR: Herbie leaned forward and listened. He was curious why Annabelle had put three red checks after his name on her notepad at school.

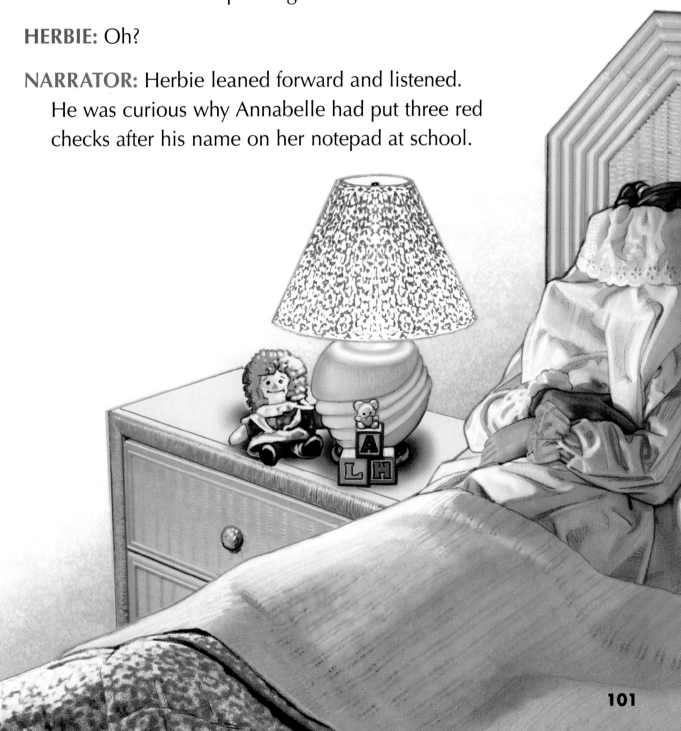

ANNABELLE: Herbie Jones wore earrings to school in October. It was Halloween, and he was supposed to be a pirate. Everyone knows a pirate wears just one *gold* earring. Herbie wore a pair of strawberries.

HERBIE: *(to himself)* That's check one.

ANNABELLE: . . . and when he wrote a story at Thanksgiving about a turkey who got his head chopped off, he called the turkey Annabelle.

HERBIE: *(Trying not to laugh, he holds up two fingers for victory.)*

ANNABELLE: *(groans)* . . . *and* he gave me a can of *salmon* for my birthday.

HERBIE: *(to himself)* Check three. What a memory she has. I better get out of here. It's getting dangerous. I've played John long enough. I'll sneeze once and then head for the door.

SFX PERSON: *(sneezes once loudly)*

ANNABELLE: But . . . Herbie Jones does have a way with words.

NARRATOR: Herbie stopped at the door.

HERBIE: Herbie Jones has a way with words?

ANNABELLE: IF YOU TELL HERBIE I SAID THAT, JOHN GREENWEED, I'LL HATE YOU FOREVER!

NARRATOR: Herbie snatched a Kleenex from the flowered box on Annabelle's desk and held it up to his mouth. This was no time to be discovered.

HERBIE: I won't. Your secret is safe with me. *(removes Kleenex and smiles)*

NARRATOR: Mr. Hodgekiss saw Herbie to the door.

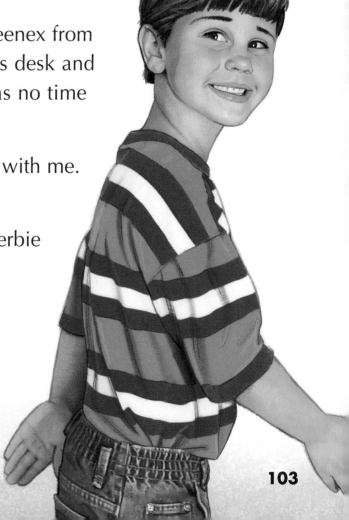

MR. HODGEKISS: Did she talk to you face to face?

HERBIE: *(feeling guilty)* No. She even thinks . . . I'm . . . John Greenweed. I kind of went along with it.

MR. HODGEKISS: Listen, Herbie, if my daughter wants to play games, you can too. Your secret is safe with me . . . John.

HERBIE: Thanks, Mr. Hodgekiss!

NARRATOR: As Herbie shuffled along the sidewalk, he kept thinking about what Annabelle had said. Herbie Jones has a way with words.

HERBIE: Is that really true? Maybe I should try making up a few more poems. Let's see . . .

Spaghetti is red.
Meatballs are brown.
You make them with eggs
And a pound of ground round.

When the sun is yellow,
It's time to play.
When the sun is red,
It's time to go to bed.

(clicks fingers) I do have a way with words!

About the Author
Suzy Kline

When she is not teaching her own students, Suzy Kline likes to talk to other students about what it is like to be a writer. She points out that not everything she has written has been accepted by publishers. "I always bring my bag of rejections," she says. This lets children know that "the first book I got published was not the first book I wrote." She also likes to show things that have given her ideas for stories—such as green slime and light-bulb necklaces.

Since she is busy teaching during most of the day, Ms. Kline does a lot of her writing early in the morning. She even writes in the bathtub!

Ms. Kline has written many award-winning stories about Herbie and Annabelle, the characters in this story. She knows them so well that she considers them almost part of her family.

Reader Response

 Open for Discussion

Would you like classmates to visit if you were home sick? Why or why not?

Comprehension Check

1. Do you think Annabelle is ashamed of the way she looks with chicken pox? Explain.

2. Herbie doesn't want to go into Annabelle's house. What are some things he says and does that give you clues?

3. This story is told like a play. Do you think it is easier or harder to read this way? Explain your answer.

4. A **cause** is why something happens. An **effect** is what happens. Why doesn't Annabelle know that Herbie is pretending to be John?

5. Herbie makes up a poem after leaving Annabelle's house. What **caused** him to do that?

Get-Well Cards

Fold a sheet of paper in half. On the inside, write a greeting you would send to someone who is sick. The greeting may be funny or serious. Decorate your card. Take turns reading your cards aloud. Then send them to a hospital or nursing home.

Character

- A **character** is a person or animal in a story.

- Authors tell us about characters when they describe what characters say, do, and feel.

Read "The Newcomer" from *Because You're Lucky* by Irene Smalls.

Talk About It

1. What actions tell you how Dawn feels about Kevin?

2. What clues give you some idea about the kind of character Dawn's mother is?

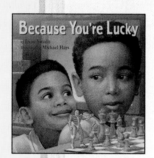

The Newcomer

by Irene Smalls

Who was going to take Hazel's boy, Kevin? Softhearted Aunt Laura was the first to say yes.

So caramel-colored Kevin with the long curly lashes came one day to live with his aunt Laura, her son, Jonathan, and her daughter, Dawn. He came without a toothbrush or a toy. He came without a change of clothes, and he came without a mommy or a daddy.

Tall teenaged Dawn answered the door.

She eyed the tiny newcomer suspiciously. "Momma, how come that raggedy little boy has to come

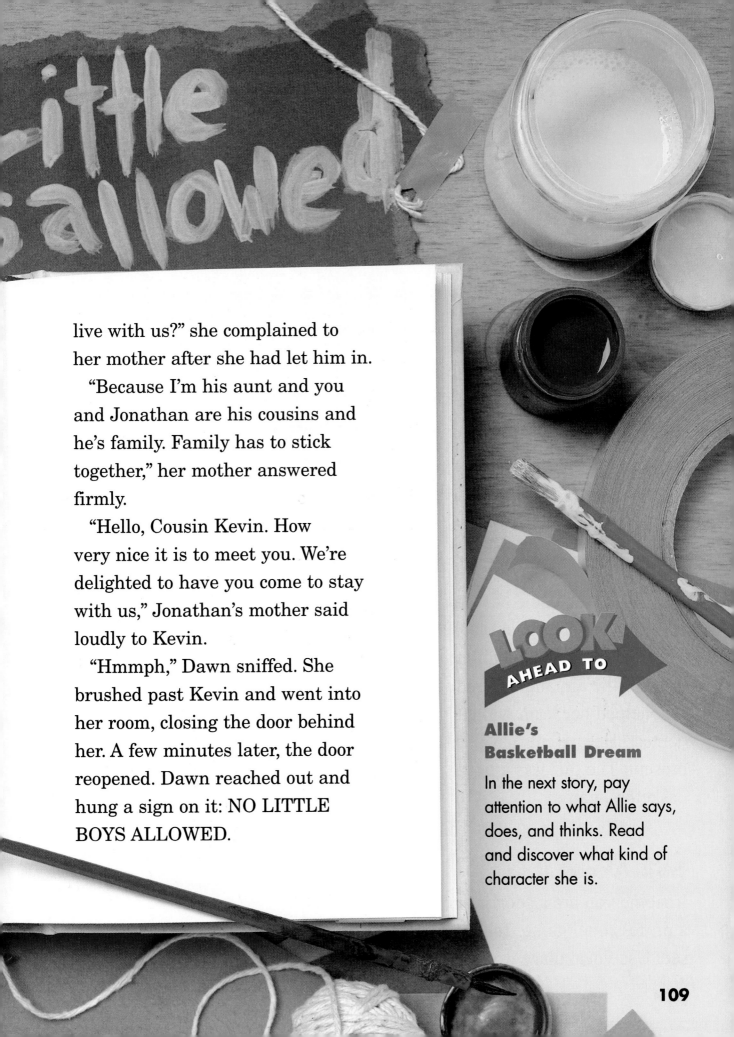

little sallowed

live with us?" she complained to her mother after she had let him in.

"Because I'm his aunt and you and Jonathan are his cousins and he's family. Family has to stick together," her mother answered firmly.

"Hello, Cousin Kevin. How very nice it is to meet you. We're delighted to have you come to stay with us," Jonathan's mother said loudly to Kevin.

"Hmmph," Dawn sniffed. She brushed past Kevin and went into her room, closing the door behind her. A few minutes later, the door reopened. Dawn reached out and hung a sign on it: NO LITTLE BOYS ALLOWED.

LOOK AHEAD TO

Allie's Basketball Dream

In the next story, pay attention to what Allie says, does, and thinks. Read and discover what kind of character she is.

Words to Know

aimed	gift	basketball
bounced	shoot	playground

Words with similar meanings, such as *big* and *large,* are **synonyms.** You can often figure out the meaning of an unknown word by finding a clue in the words around it. Sometimes this clue is a synonym.

Read this paragraph. Notice how *present* helps you understand what *gift* means?

The Winning Shot

Morgan bounced the basketball down the court. Could she shoot the winning basket? She aimed, threw the ball, watched it soar through the air, and cheered when it went in! She helped her team win the playground contest. Her parents gave her a special present. The gift was a ticket to a professional basketball game.

Talk About It

Imagine you are a sportscaster at a professional game. Tell what you see. Use vocabulary words.

by Barbara E. Barber • illustrated by Darryl Ligasan

ALLIE'S
BASKETBALL DREAM

When Allie's father came home from work Friday evening, he brought her a gift. "Because I love you," he said, and kissed Allie on her nose. The gift was something that Allie really wanted—a basketball.

The next day, Allie and her father walked to the playground. Allie loved the sound her new basketball made as she bounced it on the sidewalk. As they passed the firehouse, they waved to Mr. Puchinsky, the fire captain.

"Hi, Domino!" Allie called to the firehouse dog. Domino wagged his tail and licked Allie's basketball when she held it for him to sniff.

At the playground, Allie scanned the basketball courts while her father talked with Mr. Gonzalez, the park monitor. Some older kids already had a game going. All of the players were boys. They hardly ever missed a shot.

"Go ahead and practice, and then we'll shoot baskets together as soon as I get back from taking Aunt Harriet shopping," Allie's father told her. "I'll just be across the street. If you need me, tell Mr. Gonzalez, and he'll come get me."

"Okay," Allie replied.

She waved good-bye and ran to an empty court. She lifted her new basketball over her head and aimed. The shot missed. She aimed again. She missed again.

One of the boys playing in the next court noticed Allie and started to laugh. The others joined in.

"*Boys,*" Allie mumbled. Then she dribbled and bounced. And bounced and dribbled.

Allie's friend Keisha came into the playground with her hula hoop. Keisha saw Allie and held the hoop up. Allie aimed her basketball and . . . *Zoom!* Right through the middle.

"Let's play basketball!" Allie said.

"I don't know how," Keisha answered.

"I'll show you."

Keisha twirled her hula hoop. "My brother says basketball's a boy's game."

"Your brother doesn't know what he's talking about," Allie said.

She aimed at an empty trash can. She stepped back a few feet, and took a shot.

Thump! In!

Allie noticed her neighbor Buddy jumping rope with her friend Sheba and another girl. When he missed he ran off to join some other kids who wanted to use his volleyball.

"Hi, Allie!" Sheba called. "Is that your basketball?"

"Yep, my dad gave it to me. Want to shoot some baskets?"

"Maybe later," Sheba replied. "Want to jump double-dutch?"

"Maybe later," Allie said.

Allie pretended she was playing soccer. She kicked the ball and chased it. Then she looked up at the basket, aimed, and shot. The ball struck the backboard, then the rim, and bounded off.

Julio, who was in Allie's class at school, whizzed by on his skateboard. He made a sharp turn when he noticed the new basketball.

"Wow!" Julio exclaimed. "It that yours?"

"Yes," said Allie proudly. "Let's shoot some baskets!"

Julio looked at Allie, his eyes wide. "You must be kidding!" he said. "Me shoot baskets with a girl? No thanks!" He laughed and skated away.

Allie heaved a sigh and eyed the basket. She took another shot. The ball circled the rim and fell off. She heard some of the boys in the next court chuckle. She tried again. And again.

Allie sighed again and plopped down on a bench. Buddy walked over, bouncing his volleyball. "What's up?" he asked. "Something wrong with your basketball?"

"Well . . . " Allie hesitated.

"I'll trade you my volleyball for it! It's smaller and lighter—it'll be easier for you to play with."

"I don't know," Allie said.

Buddy reached into his pocket. He took out a miniature sports car, two quarters, and some grape bubble gum—Allie's favorite. "You can have these *and* my volleyball for the basketball," he said.

Allie thought it over. She remembered the first time her father took her to a basketball game at Madison Square Garden. She loved it all: The noise of the crowd, the bright lights on the court, and especially the slam-dunks the players made look so easy! She knew right then and there that one day, she would be a professional basketball player too. . . .

Allie hugged her basketball close. "No way I'm getting rid of this ball! It's a gift from my dad. Someday I'm going to be the best basketball player ever!"

"Well," Buddy snorted, "some guys think girls shouldn't be playin' basketball."

"That's dumb!" Allie bounced her ball. "My cousin Gwen plays on one of the best high school teams in her state. She's won more than ten trophies!"

Buddy looked surprised.

"Some girls think boys shouldn't be jumping rope," Allie continued. "They think boys are no good at it. That's dumb too."

Buddy unwrapped two pieces of gum. "Want some?"

Allie and Buddy blew huge purple bubbles. They popped their gum so loud that Domino ran over to investigate. He pranced right up to Allie and sniffed her basketball.

"Wanna play basketball, Domino? Come on, boy, let's play!"

Domino ran alongside Allie as she dribbled and bounced. Laughing, Allie turned toward the basket, and took a long-distance shot. The ball brushed against the backboard, rolled around the rim, and dropped in!

Buddy jumped up from the bench. "Nice shot, Allie!" he yelled, and ran to retrieve the ball.

"Thanks," Allie said, beaming.

Julio saw the shot too. So did Sheba. They both hurried to the center of the court.

"Here!" Allie and Julio and Sheba called to Buddy almost in one voice.

Buddy dribbled the ball, then passed it to Allie. She took a shot and missed.

"Don't worry, Allie!" Buddy yelled. Julio and Sheba each shot and missed. Allie caught the ball and dribbled closer to the basket. *I can't wait to show Dad what I can do,* she thought.

Up, up went the ball. It didn't touch the backboard.
It didn't touch the rim. It didn't touch anything.

Zoom! In!

The older boys in the next court applauded. Mr.
Gonzalez whistled. Domino barked. Above all the noise
rose a familiar voice—Allie's father.

"That-a-girl!" he shouted. "Hooray for Allie!"

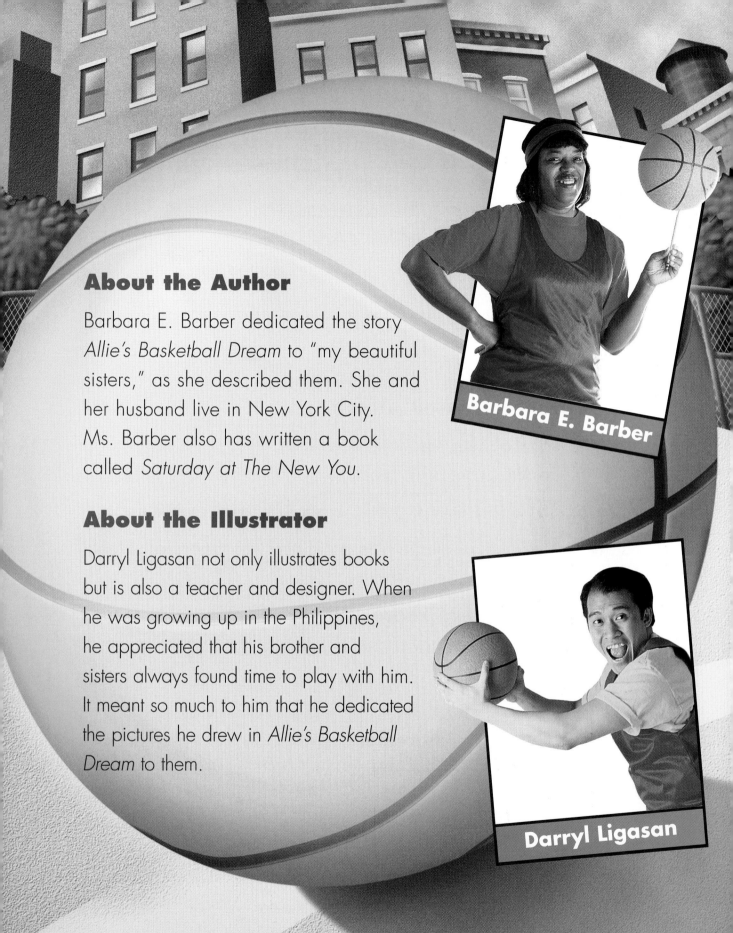

About the Author

Barbara E. Barber dedicated the story *Allie's Basketball Dream* to "my beautiful sisters," as she described them. She and her husband live in New York City. Ms. Barber also has written a book called *Saturday at The New You*.

Barbara E. Barber

About the Illustrator

Darryl Ligasan not only illustrates books but is also a teacher and designer. When he was growing up in the Philippines, he appreciated that his brother and sisters always found time to play with him. It meant so much to him that he dedicated the pictures he drew in *Allie's Basketball Dream* to them.

Darryl Ligasan

Reader Response

Open for Discussion

Pretend you are Allie's friend. What would you say or do to encourage her to keep trying?

Comprehension Check

1. How do you think Allie feels when her father gives her the basketball? Explain.

2. Why do you think Buddy wants Allie's basketball?

3. Why might Allie be pleased to hear her father's voice as she makes her final basket. Explain.

4. Allie is the main **character** in the story. She is determined. What actions or words in the story tell you what kind of person she is?

5. Allie dreams of playing professional basketball. You know what kind of **character** she is. Could she make her dream come true? Why or why not?

Sports Poem

What is your favorite sport? Write the name of your sport in a column down the left side of your paper. Now write a word or phrase that begins with each letter and tells about your sport. Share your sports poem with your classmates.

A.B.L. free-throw ace Carolyn Jones shows you

How to Sink Your Foul Shots

written by Andrea N. Whittaker
photographed by Manny Millan

Reading Across Texts

Reading a Magazine Article

✓ **Read the main article first.** It will give you background for the pictures.

✓ **Then read the captions— words next to, over, or under the pictures.** They will explain what you see and may help explain parts of the article.

Focus Your Reading

This magazine article gives tips for shooting foul shots. As you read, think about how these tips might help Allie shoot better.

A foul shot is also called a free throw. Why? Because no one guards you when you shoot. Sinking a 15-foot free throw looks easy. But it takes a lot of work to make the shot when you are tired and the game is on the line.

Carolyn Jones is a 5 foot 9 inch guard. She is an excellent foul shooter because she has proper technique, she concentrates, and she is confident.

"You have to be confident that you'll make the shot every time," says Carolyn. "You can't think, 'Oh, my gosh, what if I miss?!' Then you *will* miss! Say to yourself, 'The ball is going in!' "

Here are some of Carolyn's free-throw tips.

The Shot

- **Shoot every free throw with the same motion.**
- **Release the ball when you are on your tiptoes.**
- **Snap your wrist forward, to give the ball backspin.**
- **Stay on your toes until the ball drops into the net.**

129

Drills

Here are three drills to help you learn to release the ball properly.

Lying on Your Back

Shoot the ball so that it goes two or three feet straight up and straight back down. Snap your wrist as you release the ball.

Phone Booth

Imagine you are shooting up and out of a phone booth. Use one hand. This helps put the ball over the rim.

Chair Shot

When you shoot from a chair, you can't use your legs to help push the ball. Concentrate on your arms and wrists. Keep your shoulders facing the basket.

The Perfect Free Throw

If you are right-handed, stand with your right foot slightly forward. (Reverse the stance if you are left-handed.)

Get a feel for the basketball. I like to dribble three times before I shoot.

Hold the ball with your fingertips. Bend your shooting arm in an "L" shape. Place your nonshooting hand on the side of the ball to hold it in place.

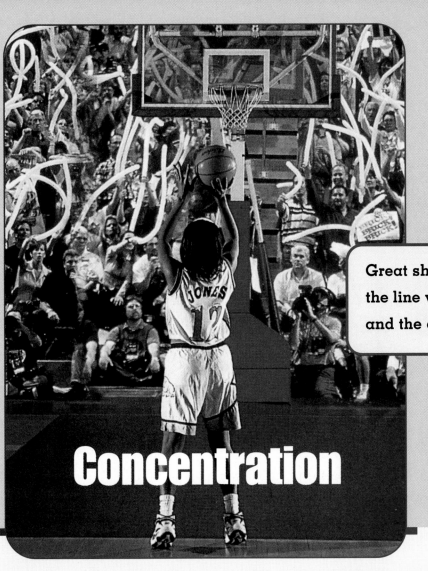

Concentration

Great shooters love going to the line when the game is close and the crowd is going wild.

Focus on your shooting form. Tell yourself that the ball is going in!

Bend your knees a bit. Look at the entire basket, not just the front of the rim.

Lift the ball smoothly as you begin to straighten up. Tuck in the elbow of your shooting arm.

Extend your shooting arm. Snap your wrist. Don't jump. Release the ball when you're on your tiptoes.

131

My Brother Is as Generous as Anyone Could Be

by Jack Prelutsky

My brother is as generous
as anyone could be,
for everything he's ever had
he's always shared with me.
He has loaned me his binoculars,
his new computer games,
and his wind-up walking dragon
that breathes artificial flames.

I've been grateful for his robots,
for his giant teddy bear,
but not for certain other things
I'd hoped he'd never share—
Though I'm glad he's shared his rockets
and his magic jumping rocks,
I wish my brother hadn't shared
his case of chicken pox.

Summer Vacation

by Karama Fufuka

We read books in school
and we write stories
about what we did on
summer vacations.

This summer,
I played ball
and went to the beach
and Mama brought home
a brand-new baby.

Poem

by Langston Hughes

I loved my friend.
He went away from me.
There's nothing more to say.
The poem ends,
Soft as it began—
I loved my friend.

Watering

by Alma Flor Ada

Your smiles
to your friends
are like water
to growing plants.

Regar

por Alma Flor Ada

Tus sonrisas son
para tus amigos
como el riego
para las plantas.

August afternoon
by Marion Edey

Where shall we go?
   What shall we play?
What shall we do
   On a hot summer day?

We'll sit in the swing.
   Go low. Go high.
And drink lemonade
   Till the glass is dry.

One straw for you,
   One straw for me,
In the cool green shade
   Of the walnut tree.

THE WHOLE WIDE WORLD

How can we learn about and care for the world?

Graphic Sources

- A **graphic source** can be a picture, diagram, map, chart, graph, or something else that shows information.

- Graphic sources are useful because they show lots of information in an easy-to-see way.

- Making your own graphic, such as a chart, picture, or diagram, can help you understand what you read.

Read "Flowering Plants" from *What's Inside of Plants?* by Herbert S. Zim.

Talk About It

1. How does the diagram of the flowering plant help you understand the paragraph?

2. Look at the diagram. What parts of the plant shown do we usually eat?

FLOWERING PLANTS

by Herbert S. Zim

There are thousands of kinds of plants. Some are so small you can hardly see them. Other plants are the largest living things. The kinds of plants we see most often are the flowering plants. Peas, beans, corn, roses, and tomatoes are flowering plants. Most trees are flowering plants too. All flowering plants have leaves. They also have stems, roots, flowers, and fruits. Some are woody and grow for many years. Some grow one year and bloom the next. Some live and die in a single summer.

Flower

Seed

Leaf

Fruit

Stem

Roots

Bean Plant

LOOK AHEAD TO

Fly Traps! Plants That Bite Back

In the next selection, you will learn about plants that eat insects. Read and use the pictures to help you understand these plants.

Vocabulary

Words to Know

collect	pitcher	hinge
plants	insects	trap

When you read, you may come across a word you don't know. To figure out its meaning, look for clues around it. A clue might be found in the details or examples given near the unknown word.

Notice how *hinge* is used in the sentences below. Find details or examples in the same sentence. What do you think *hinge* means?

Surprising Plant

As I fill a pitcher with water to feed the plants, I notice insects crawling on the leaves of the Venus flytrap. The flytrap leaf has sticky hairs that feel an insect crawling. Then, just like a door with a hinge, the leaf closes down on the insect to trap it. I want to collect more of these interesting plants!

Talk About It

Would you want a Venus flytrap? Tell a friend why or why not. Use vocabulary words.

FLY TRAPS!

Plants That Bite Back

by Martin Jenkins / illustrated by David Parkins

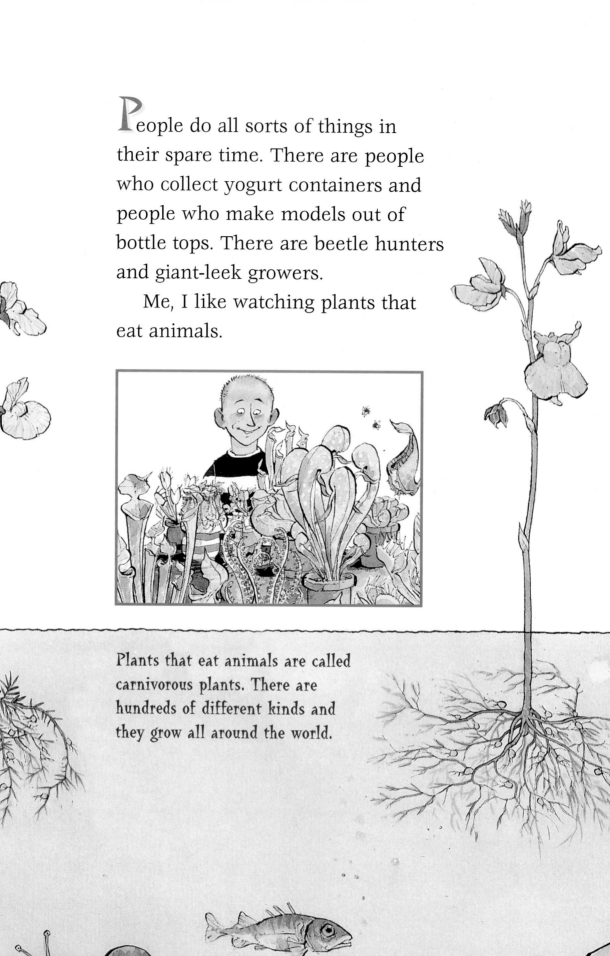

People do all sorts of things in their spare time. There are people who collect yogurt containers and people who make models out of bottle tops. There are beetle hunters and giant-leek growers.

Me, I like watching plants that eat animals.

Plants that eat animals are called carnivorous plants. There are hundreds of different kinds and they grow all around the world.

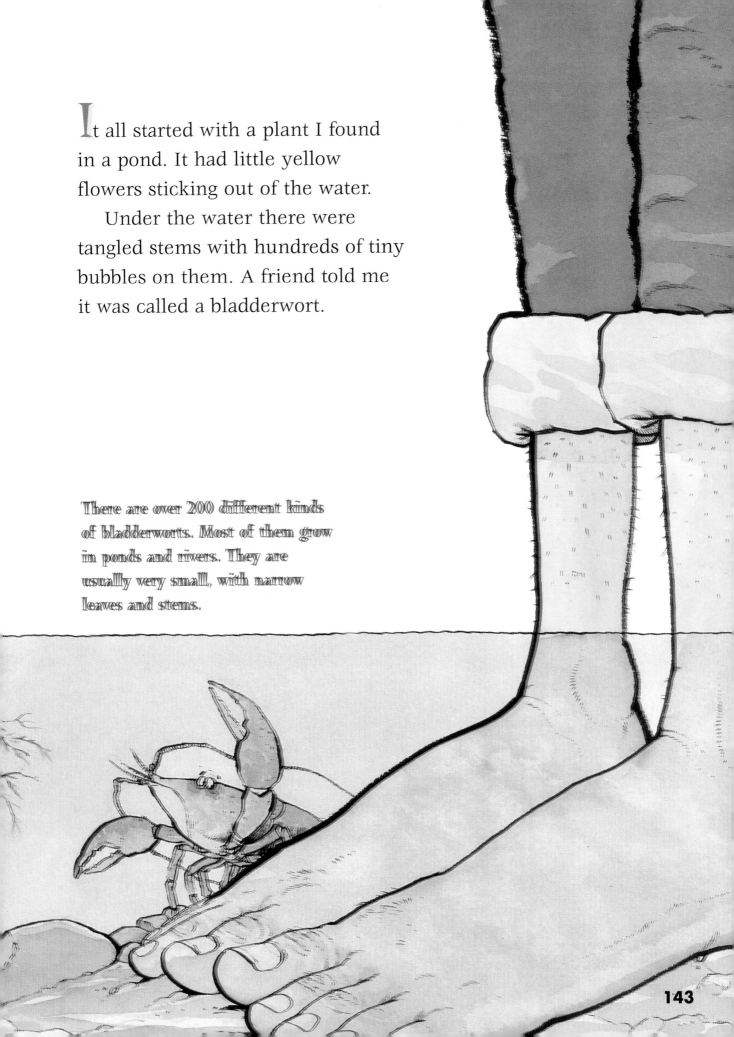

It all started with a plant I found in a pond. It had little yellow flowers sticking out of the water.

Under the water there were tangled stems with hundreds of tiny bubbles on them. A friend told me it was called a bladderwort.

There are over 200 different kinds of bladderworts. Most of them grow in ponds and rivers. They are usually very small, with narrow leaves and stems.

She said the bubbles on the stems were the bladders. Each one had a trap door shut tight, with little trigger hairs around it.

Whenever a water flea or other bug touched a hair, the trap door swung back and in the bug went.

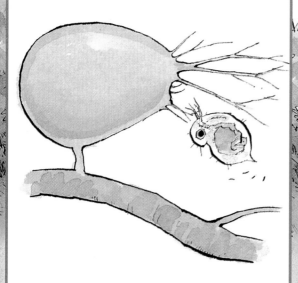

To set its traps, a bladderwort sucks the water out of its bladders.

When a trap door opens, water rushes in, dragging the bug in with it.

Then the trap door slammed shut and there was no way out. And it all happened in the blink of an eye.

The bladderwort oozes special chemicals into the bladder. These dissolve the bug and the plant sucks it up.

Wow, that's neat, I thought. The trouble was, the traps on my plant were so small and so quick that I couldn't really see them work.

Well, I decided, I'll just have to find a bigger carnivorous plant.

So I did.

I had to climb a mountain, mind you, and walk through all its boggiest, mossiest places.

But there in the moss were little red plants, shining in the sun. I thought they were covered in dewdrops, but they weren't. They were sundews, and the shiny parts were sticky like honey. I'm sure you can guess what they were for.

When a bug gets stuck on a sundew, the leaf slowly curls up around it.

Then the soft parts of the bug are dissolved by chemicals and eaten.

I had to leave the sundews when the clouds rolled in. But as soon as I got home, I sent away for some sundew seeds of my own.

Afterward, the leaf opens up again and the leftover bug parts fall off.

Butterworts are carnivorous plants, too, and often grow in the same places as sundews. They have flat leaves like flypaper. Little bugs stick to the leaves and slowly dissolve.

The seeds weren't just for ordinary sundews, though. They were for Giant African sundews. I sowed them in a pot of moss and covered it with glass.

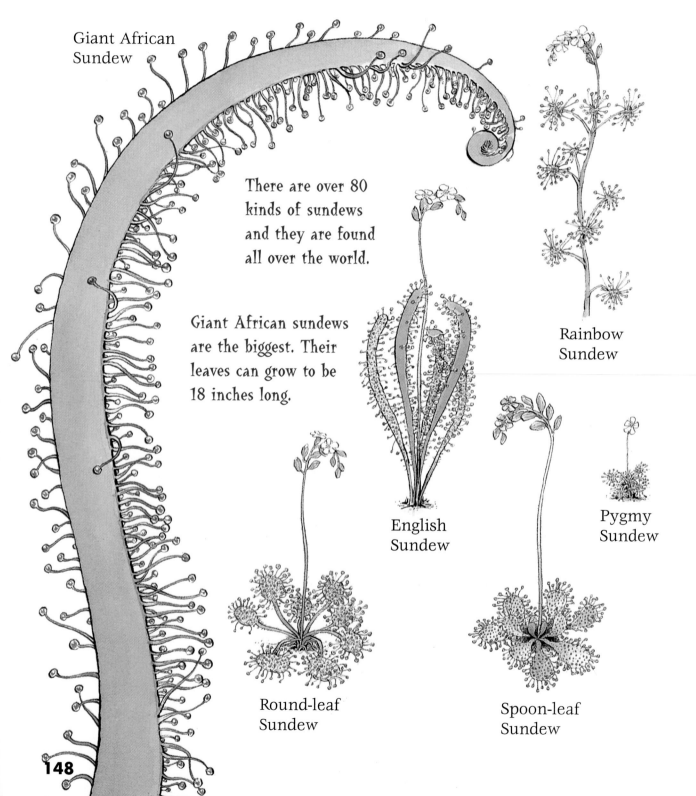

Giant African Sundew

There are over 80 kinds of sundews and they are found all over the world.

Giant African sundews are the biggest. Their leaves can grow to be 18 inches long.

Rainbow Sundew

English Sundew

Pygmy Sundew

Round-leaf Sundew

Spoon-leaf Sundew

I watered the pot every day with rainwater straight from the water tank. Soon the seeds started to sprout and I had dozens of baby sundews.

They grew and grew, until they were almost big enough to start catching things.

Then one day I watered them with the wrong kind of water—and every single one died.

I gave up on sundews after that, but I did grow a Venus flytrap. It lived on the windowsill and caught insects. Each of its leaves had a hinge down the center, several little trigger hairs, and a spiky rim.

When a fly or a wasp walked over a leaf, it was perfectly safe if it didn't touch any of the hairs. It was even safe if it touched just one of the hairs. But if it touched two of the hairs, then . . .

My sundews died because I accidentally put fertilizer in the water. All carnivorous plants hate fertilizer.

Venus flytraps grow in only one small part of the southeastern United States. They are rare now because people have drained many of the marshes where they once lived.

Small insects such as ants can escape from a Venus flytrap—they're not big enough to be worth eating.

But flies and wasps are a different story. Once caught, the more they struggle the tighter the leaf presses together.

When the leaf is fully closed, it begins to dissolve its victim.

151

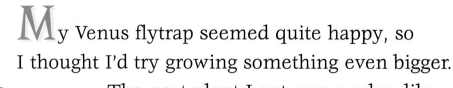My Venus flytrap seemed quite happy, so I thought I'd try growing something even bigger. The next plant I got was a cobra lily. This one caught insects, too, but it didn't actually do very much. It had leaves like funnels, with a slippery rim and a little pool at the bottom. When insects crawled inside, they fell into the pool and couldn't climb out. So they stayed there and became bug soup for the lily.

Cobra lilies get their name because their leaves look like cobras, not because they eat them!

152

I was very happy with my cobra lily. Surely it was the biggest carnivorous plant of all. But then my friend told me about pitcher plants.

Pitchers are even bigger, she said, but they are very difficult to grow. In that case, I thought, I'll just go and find some wild ones.

So I went—

all the way to Malaysia.

Cobra lilies grow along the western coast of the United States. Their leaves can be up to 18 inches long.

And there, growing up the trees at the edge
of the jungle, were hundreds of pitcher plants.
Fat red ones, thin yellow ones, curly green ones,
all waiting for flies.

I didn't see the biggest pitcher plant of all,
though. It's called the Rajah pitcher plant and it
grows on the tallest mountain in Borneo.

It has pitchers the size of footballs. People say
it can even catch some kinds of squirrels, but I'm
not convinced.

Pitcher plants are found
in tropical countries. Like
most other carnivorous
plants, they usually grow
where there is hardly any soil
or where the soil is very poor.

The pitchers' leaves look like
vases, and they catch insects
in the same way that cobra
lilies do.

There are some kinds of
spiders, and even some small
tree frogs, that are able to live
inside the pitchers. They cling
to the slippery sides and grab
the insects that fall in.

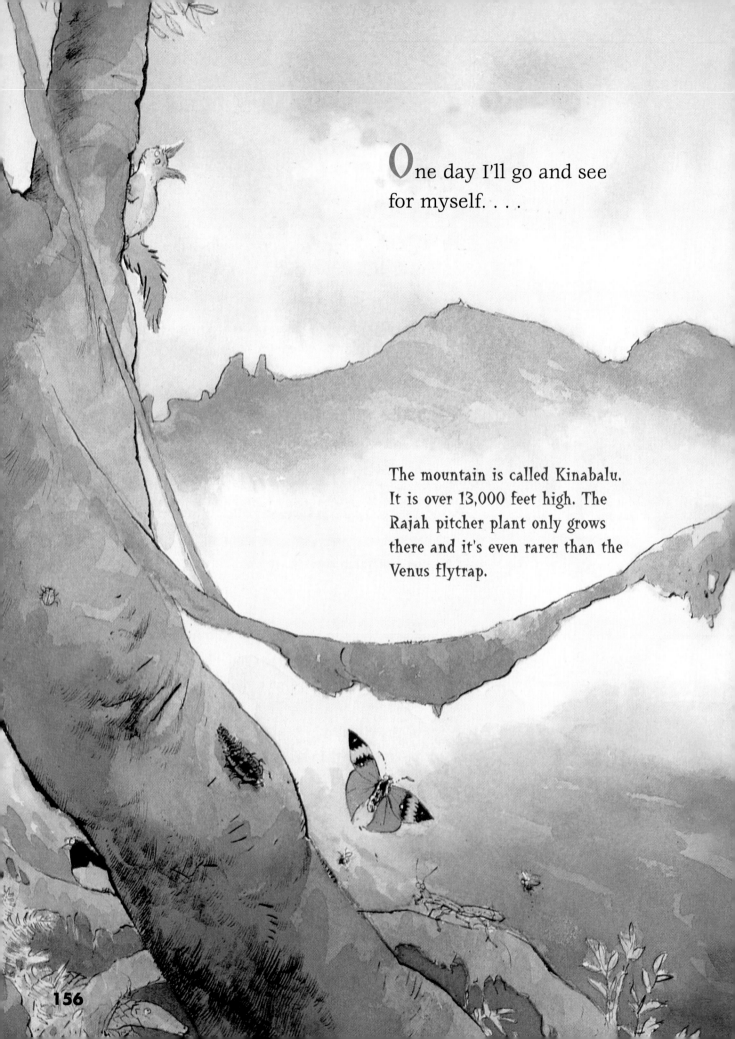

One day I'll go and see
for myself. . . .

The mountain is called Kinabalu.
It is over 13,000 feet high. The
Rajah pitcher plant only grows
there and it's even rarer than the
Venus flytrap.

About the Author
Martin Jenkins

Fly Traps! Plants That Bite Back is one of Martin Jenkins's first books for children. "It is absolutely autobiographical," Mr. Jenkins says about the book. He really travels to faraway jungles in search of unusual plants. Mr. Jenkins is a conservation biologist who writes articles for the World Wildlife Federation. He also is the author of *Wings, Stings and Wriggly Things.*

About the Illustrator
David Parkins

Drawing the pictures for *Fly Traps! Plants That Bite Back* brought back memories for David Parkins. "When I first started out as an illustrator," he says, "I did a book on wildlife and spent a year tramping around fields drawing berries and birds. So in a way, this book takes me back to my roots." Mr. Parkins has illustrated many other children's books. He lives in England.

Reader Response

Open for Discussion

Which kind of plant in *Fly Traps!*
Plants That Bite Back was the
most interesting to you? Why?

Comprehension Check

1. Think of one word to describe the narrator. Find parts of the text that support your choice.

2. What is the most important way in which all the plants in the selection are alike? Explain.

3. Some of the pictures and text are funny. Is this a good way to present information? Tell why you think as you do.

4. Use the pictures on pages 144 and 145 as a **graphic source** to tell a friend how the bladderwort captures its food. Use your hands as well as your voice.

5. Find the **graphic source** that shows how the cobra lily got its name. Tell how the plant and animal are alike.

Grandpa's Advice

With a partner pretend to be Grandpa Fly and Junior Fly. Have Grandpa explain to Junior how to be safe around Venus flytraps. Junior can ask questions. Then trade parts with your partner and have Grandpa give a warning about pitcher plants.

158

Can You Catch Flies?

by Rhonda Lucas Donald

A real pitcher plant catches lots of flies. If you follow these directions, you can make your own pitcher plant. Then see if you can catch flies too.

What You Need

- 6-inch x 9-inch piece of thin cardboard (about the thickness of a manila folder)
- 11-inch piece of thin string or thread
- scissors
- two strips of paper, each 3/4 inch x 4 inches
- pen or pencil
- white glue
- tape (optional)
- crayons, markers, or paints and paintbrushes

Reading a How-to Article

✓ **Read all directions first.** You will know step-by-step how long it will take or how hard your project will be.

✓ **Gather materials needed.** Have everything you need before starting.

✓ **Follow directions carefully.** If you want what you're making to turn out right, be sure to do exactly what you read.

Focus Your Reading

This how-to article shows how to make a paper pitcher plant. As you read, think about how a real pitcher plant traps a fly.

What You Do

1. Trace the pitcher-plant pattern. Paste it onto a piece of thin cardboard and cut it out.
2. Color one side of the cutout to look like the inside of the plant. Color the outside bright green.
3. To make the hairs that line the inside of pitcher plants, fold the strips of white paper in half lengthwise. Cut slits in one half of each strip (see drawing A).
4. Apply a line of glue to the uncut side of each strip and carefully glue the "hairs" to the inside of the plant (see pattern). Make sure that the hairs point toward the bottom. (In real pitcher plants, the hairs make it hard for the flies to crawl back out.)
5. Roll the cut out pitcher plant into a cone shape (see drawing B). Tape or glue the edges of the cone together.

6. Tape or glue one end of the string to the inside front lip of the pitcher plant (see drawing B).

7. Trace the shapes with the flies on them. Glue each one to a piece of cardboard, draw flies on them, and cut them both out.

8. Glue the flies back-to-back onto the loose end of the string. Let them dry.

9. Now your pitcher plant is ready to catch flies! Just flip the fly up and try to get it into the pitcher.

10. When you get good at catching flies, curl the plant's "hood" down to partly cover the pitcher's opening. (Roll the hood over your finger and hold it in place for a couple of seconds.) Can your pitcher plant *still* catch its dinner?

pattern

glue strips here

hood

B

tape

roll paper into cone

Realism and Fantasy

- A **realistic story** tells about something that could happen in real life.

- A **fantasy** has some things that could happen and some things that could not happen.

Read "Under the Umbrella" from *The Willow Umbrella* by Christine Widman and "The Naughty Umbrella" from *Roger's Umbrella* by Daniel Pinkwater.

Write About It

1. In columns labeled *realistic* and *fantasy,* write story details that show whether the story is realistic or a fantasy.

2. Which story is realistic and which is a fantasy? Tell why you think so.

UNDER
the Umbrella

by Christine Widman

Ashley sees Rebecca coming down the street. She's holding a yellow umbrella. It looks like the sun Ashley painted in her picture. She wishes Rebecca were bringing the sun so they could play dolls under the willow tree.

Rain, rain go away. Ashley wants to play.

She waves to Rebecca. "Hurry up . . . come in. We have to play inside today."

"No we don't. Come out! Let's walk in the rain."

Ashley squeezes close to Rebecca under the yellow umbrella. The air is wet and warm. The sidewalk is shiny like a gray satin sash.

THE NAUGHTY
Umbrella

by Daniel Pinkwater

When Roger left for school on rainy days, or days that looked like they might be rainy, his mother always said to him, "Roger, be sure to take your umbrella."

He didn't like taking his umbrella. For one thing, it got in the way. And for another, he didn't like the way the umbrella behaved.

Sometimes the umbrella would suddenly turn itself inside out for no reason.

Sometimes it would catch a gust of wind and make Roger walk on tiptoe.

Sometimes it would even lift him completely off the ground.

But that was nothing compared to what the umbrella would do at night.

It would suddenly pop open and hop around the room. It would flap like a big bird or bat. It would try to escape out the window.

Roger would have to grab the umbrella and struggle with it until he could finally stuff it into his closet, where it would thump and flap for hours.

LOOK AHEAD TO

Guys from Space

In the next story, guys from space take an Earth boy on a journey. Could it be real? Is it a fantasy? Read and find out.

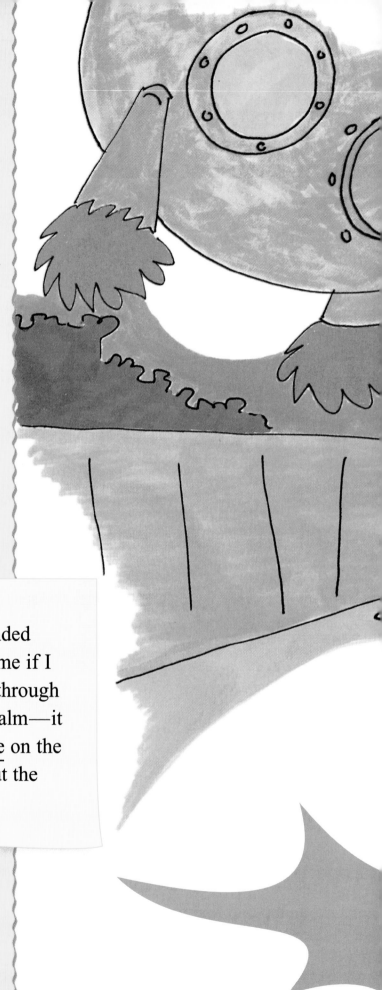

Vocabulary

Words to Know

breathe   planet   space
dream   scary   spaceship

Words with opposite meaning, like *hot* and *cold,* are called **antonyms.** You can often figure out the meaning of a word you don't know by finding a clue in the words around it. Sometimes this clue is an antonym.

Read this paragraph. Notice how *calm* helps you understand what *scary* means.

Was It Just a Dream?

I had a great dream! A spaceship landed outside my window. An alien asked me if I wanted to go to his planet. We flew through space at top speed. The trip wasn't calm—it was scary! What if I couldn't breathe on the strange planet? Just when I found out the planet was safe . . . I woke up!

Write About It

Imagine you traveled to another planet. Write a postcard home. Use some vocabulary words.

164

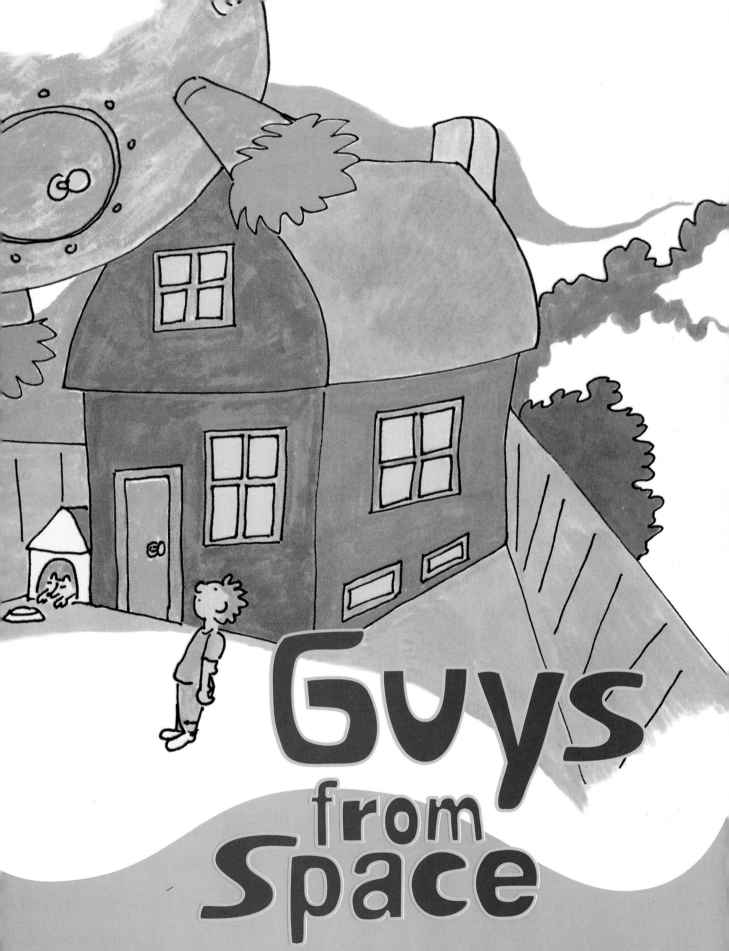

Guys
from
Space

written and illustrated by **Daniel Pinkwater**

I was in the backyard.

I wasn't doing anything.

There was something in the sky.

I looked up.

There was something big up there.

It was not a bird.

It was not an airplane.

It was not a balloon.

It was not a cloud.

It was something from space.

It was neat!

It was coming down.

It was coming down into the yard!

It did not make a noise.

It landed like a dream.

"This is good!" I said.

I was not scared.

When the thing from space had landed, a little door opened.

Guys from space came out.

They were no bigger than me.

"Is this Chicago?" they asked me.

"This is my yard," I said.

The guys from space talked to each other.

"Kid, would you like to come for a ride?"

"No!" I said.

"You don't want to come?"

"No."

"It will be fun," the space guys said. "We will bring you back."

"Nothing doing," I said.

"You will be the first Earth person to ride in our spaceship," they said.

"I am not allowed to go with anybody," I said. "Unless my mother or father says I can."

"Are your mother or father the same size as you?" the guys from space asked.

"Bigger," I said.

"Then they will not fit. Just you come."

"I have to ask my mother," I said.

"Is she scary?" the space guys wanted to know.

"Not very."

"All right, ask her. Where is she?"

"She's in the house," I said. "Wait here."

I went inside the house.

My mother was in the basement.

She was weaving.

She weaves.

She was weaving some sort of rug.

She has this loom.

It's what you weave on.

"There are some space guys in the yard," I said.

"That's nice," my mother said.

"Is it all right if I go up in the spaceship?"

"Sure," my mother said.

"Do you want to see the space guys?"

"Not right now, dear," my mother said. "I'm just doing the hard part of this rug."

"Then I can just go with them?"

"If you aren't late for supper."

"I'll see you later," I said.

"Have a good time," my mother said.

I went out into the yard.

"She says I can go," I said.

"Good!" the guys from space said.
"Get your space helmet."

"I don't have one," I said.

"No space helmet? That's too bad."

"Don't you have an extra one?" I asked.

"Afraid not."

"Then I can't go?"

"Well, you have to have a space helmet."

"Oh," I said.

"Maybe we could fix something up. What's that?"

"That's the dog's water bowl," I said.

"What's that stuff in it?"

"Water," I said.

"Could you dump it out?" they asked.

"I guess so," I said. "Would that work as
a space helmet?"

"Try it on," the space guys said.

I tried it on. "It's cold," I said. "How does it look?"

"It looks good," the space guys said. "Come on."

"Why do I have to wear this?" I asked.

"You have to. It's a rule. Let's go."

We went through the little door.

The space guys turned knobs.

They pushed buttons.

They switched switches.

Something buzzed.

Something beeped.

Something whistled.

"Here we go," the space guys said. "Look out the window."

I looked out the window.

We were going up.

"Isn't this neat?" the space guys said.

We were going fast.

"Where are we going?" I asked.

"We will visit some other planet," the space guys said.

"Will I be home in time for supper?" I asked.

"What time is supper?"

"Six."

"Easy."

"I thought other planets were far away," I said.

"They are."

"How can we go to another planet and be back by six?"

"Easy. We go fast. Hold on."

The spaceship went faster.

It went very fast.

It went very, very fast.

It went faster than sound.

It went faster than light.

I didn't like it.

"This is too fast," I said.

"Never mind. We have come to a planet," the space guys said.

"What planet is this?" I asked.

"Who knows? Some planet," the guys from space said. "Let's get out and look around."

"How do you know if there is air on this planet?" I asked.

"If there is no air, you can't breathe," the space guys said.

"Then what?" I asked.

"Then we run back into the spaceship and close the door," the guys from space said.

"How about wild animals and bad people?" I asked.

"Same thing. We run back inside."

"It sounds simple."

"We are space guys. We know what we are doing."

The space guys opened the door, and we went outside.

"The air is good," the space guys said.

"I don't see any wild animals," I said.

"No, this is a good planet. We can tell," the space guys said.

"What do we do now?" I asked.

"We look around. We explore."

We looked around.

It was a neat planet.

There were a lot of rocks.

I picked one up.

"Put me down!" the rock said.

I put it down.

"The rock talked," I said.

"Hello, rock," the space guys said. "We like your planet."

"Who are you?" the rock asked.

"We are guys from space," the space guys said. "We are just visiting."

"Oh, that's all right," the rock said. "Look around and have a nice time."

"Thank you," the space guys said. "Is there anything special here? Something we should see?"

"There is a root beer stand," the rock said.

"Oh, good! We like root beer," the space guys said.

"Do you like root beer?" they asked me.

"Sure," I said.

"Where is the root beer stand?" they asked the rock.

"It is there, behind that big rock," the rock said.

We went to the root beer stand.

It was nice.

It had lots of lights.

Space things were drinking root beer.

There was a big space thing in the root beer stand.

He was ugly, in a nice way.

"Five root beers, please," the guys from space said.

"You have money?" the big space thing said.

"We have plastic fish," the space guys said. "We use plastic fish for money."

"Plastic fish are fine," the big space thing said. "Five root beers for five plastic fish."

"On our planet, we get ten root beers for five plastic fish," the space guys said.

"Do you get ice cream in the root beers?" the big space thing asked.

"No. We never heard of ice cream in root beer," the space guys said.

"Five plastic fish for five root beers with ice cream," the big space thing said.

The space guys gave the space thing five plastic fish.

"Ice cream in root beer," they said. "What a strange idea!"

The big space thing gave us the root beers with ice cream.

"This is good," the space guys said. "We will teach the people on our own planet about this."

I drank my root beer.

I ate the ice cream with a spoon.

I looked at the space things having root beer.

It was good root beer.

"Hurry and finish," the space guys said.

"We have to go?" I asked.

"We want to go to our own planet. We want to tell our people about ice cream in root beer. We want to go back and tell them before someone else does."

"You will take me home first?" I said.

"Yes. Now finish your root beer and ice cream."

I finished my root beer and ice cream.

We got into the spaceship.

The space guys took me home.

We landed in the backyard.

"Do you want to come in?" I asked the space guys. "Do you want to meet my mother?"

"Not now," the space guys said. "We want to go home. We want to tell our people."

"You want to tell them about root beer and ice cream."

"Yes! Our people will like it. We will be heroes."

"Thank you for the ride, and the root beer," I said.

"You are welcome," the space guys said.

"Good-bye."

"Good-bye."

The spaceship took off.

I went into the house.

"Why do you have the dog's water bowl on your head?" my mother asked.

"I used it for a space helmet," I said.

"Fill it with water and put it back," my mother said. "The dog may want a drink. Then wash your hands and face and come to supper."

"I took a ride in a spaceship," I said.

"That's nice, dear," my mother said. "Did you have a good time?"

"The space guys bought me a root beer," I said.

"I hope you thanked them," my mother said.

"I did," I said.

Daniel Manus Pinkwater

When Daniel Manus Pinkwater was a young boy, he and his friends acted out the adventure stories they read. One day they would act out the story *20,000 Leagues Under the Sea.* The next day they might act out *The Three Musketeers.* He and his friends would tell each other about books they liked.

Now that Mr. Pinkwater is grown up, he creates his own adventure stories. He often draws the pictures for them too. Unusual things happen in his stories, such as a train car turning into a time machine and a blue moose getting a job as a waiter.

Even though amusing things happen in Mr. Pinkwater's stories, he is very serious about what he does. "I think children's books are the most important thing you can do," he says, "because these are people who are learning about reading."

Reader Response

If guys from space landed at your house, would you want to go for a ride with them? Tell why or why not.

Comprehension Check

1. Is the space guys' plan to see whether a planet's air is okay a good one? Why or why not?

2. Why does the boy wear the dog's dish as a helmet? Does the dog dish do anything that a real helmet does?

3. Does the boy's mother think he has gone on a ride in a spaceship? Explain your answer.

4. *Guys from Space* is a **fantasy** because many things that happen in the story could not really happen. Name two events from the story that could not really happen.

5. Some events in a **fantasy** could really happen. Which character seems to do only real things? What are these things?

Magazine Article

Pretend you are the boy who went up with the guys from space. Write a short article for a travel magazine telling about your trip. Include interesting details.

Context Clues

- To figure out the meaning of a word, use **context clues.**

- Often a context clue defines or explains the word. Look in the sentences or paragraph around the word.

- You may need to use a dictionary or glossary to check the meaning of the word.

Read "Stormy Weather" from *Weather* by Martha Ryan.

Talk About It

1. Tell what words or sentences help you understand the meanings of these words: *hurricane, eye,* and *tornado.*

2. Look up each word in the glossary. Do the definitions give you more or less information than the context clues in "Stormy Weather"?

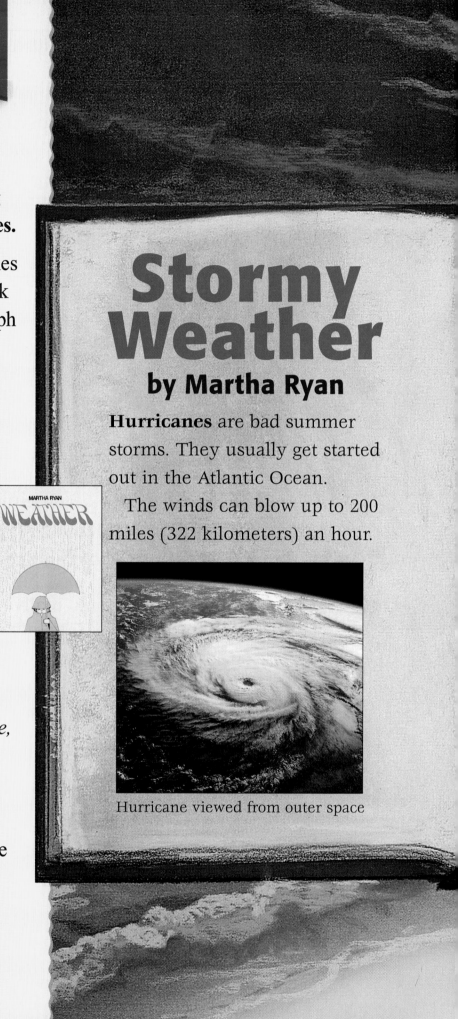

Stormy Weather

by Martha Ryan

Hurricanes are bad summer storms. They usually get started out in the Atlantic Ocean.

The winds can blow up to 200 miles (322 kilometers) an hour.

Hurricane viewed from outer space

They blow around in a circle. In the center it is very calm. This is called the **eye** of the storm.

In the Pacific Ocean, hurricanes are called **typhoons** (tie-FOONZ).

Tornadoes are another kind of storm.

They are small but very bad. You see them as a dark column coming down from a big storm cloud. The column is really a circle of wind that is blowing very fast.

A tornado rips up everything in its path.

Tornadoes usually form over big flat pieces of land.

LOOK AHEAD TO

Tornado Alert

In the next selection, you will read more about tornadoes. Use context clues to help you understand words you may not know.

Words to Know

destroy   storms   noise

warnings   powerful   wrecked

Words with similar meanings, like *dish* and *plate*, are **synonyms.** You can often figure out the meaning of a word you don't know by finding a clue in the words around it. Sometimes this clue is a synonym.

Read this paragraph. Notice how *smash* helps you understand what *destroy* means.

Wild Weather

A loud noise and winds with blowing dust are two warnings of a tornado. Tornadoes are storms that are very powerful. They can smash windows and cars and destroy homes. They can pull trees out of the ground. If a tornado is coming, go to your basement or a room without windows. Your house may be wrecked, but you will be safe.

Talk About It

Think of a sentence about a tornado that uses some vocabulary words. Share your sentence with the class.

TORNADO ALERT

by Franklyn M. Branley

Tornadoes are powerful storms.

On a tornado day the air is hot and still. Clouds build up rapidly. They get thick and dark. In the distance there is thunder and lightning, rain and hail.

Here and there parts of the clouds seem to reach toward the ground. Should these parts grow larger and become funnel shaped, watch out. The funnels could become tornadoes.

The funnel of a tornado is usually dark gray or black. It may also be yellowish or red.

The colors come from red and yellow dirt picked up by the tornado as it moves along the ground.

Tornadoes can strike almost anywhere, but usually they happen where there is a lot of flat land. Most tornadoes occur in Texas, Oklahoma, Kansas, Nebraska, Iowa, and Missouri. Florida also has a lot of tornadoes.

Tornadoes can touch down over seas and lakes. When that happens, they are called waterspouts.

Most tornadoes occur during April, May, and June. That's when cold air meets warm air near the Earth's surface. The cold air pushes under the warm air. The warm air is lighter than the cold air and rises rapidly.

As the warm air moves upward, it spins around, or twists. That's why tornadoes are sometimes called twisters. Some people call them cyclones. The wind speed around the funnel of the tornado may reach 300 miles an hour. No other wind on Earth blows that fast.

As the hot air rises, it also spreads out. It makes a funnel of air, with the small part of the funnel touching the ground and the large part in the dark clouds. Air all around the tornado moves in toward the funnel. At the same time, storm winds push the twisting funnel, moving it along the Earth.

During tornado season in the United States, there may be 40 or 50 tornadoes in one week. Sometimes there are many more. Most are small. Usually a tornado blows itself out in less than an hour. Some last only a few seconds.

Small tornadoes don't travel far, and they cause little damage. Big tornadoes destroy everything in their paths. They may travel two hundred miles and last several hours.

During a tornado there is thunder and lightning, rain and hail. And there is lots of noise. It can sound as loud as a freight train or a jet engine. The word *tornado* comes from a Latin word that means "thunder." Some of the noise does come from thunder, but most of it comes from the roaring wind. There is lots of noise, and lots and lots of wind.

Tornadoes are very powerful, and some cause a lot of damage. Tornadoes can pick up branches and boards, stones and bricks, cars, and sometimes even people.

They can rip off roofs and leave a trail of wrecked houses. A tornado's path may be only 20 or 30 feet wide. Or it might be 1000 feet or more—maybe even a mile.

In 1931 a tornado in Minnesota lifted a train off its tracks. The train and its passengers were carried through the air and dropped 80 feet from the tracks. There were 170 people on board. Though many people were hurt, only one person was killed. But in 1974 a series of tornadoes in Missouri, Illinois, Indiana, and ten other states killed 315 people in twenty-four hours.

Scientists keep a close watch during tornado season. They use satellites that see storms developing. And there is radar to detect tornadoes.

Tornado spotters are people who watch for tornadoes. They tell radio and television stations to warn people about tornadoes while the twisters are still far away. The warnings tell people to go to a safe spot, where the tornado can't hurt them.

If a tornado is on its way, here's what you should do. Go to a nearby storm cellar. Storm cellars are underground rooms with heavy doors. They are safe.

If you are in a mobile home, get out of it. A tornado can rip apart a mobile home, even when it is tied down with strong cables. Lie facedown in a ditch and cover your head with your hands. When you're in a ditch, sticks and stones flying through the air can't hit you.

If you are in a house, go to the basement and crouch under the stairs or under a heavy workbench. Or go to a closet that is far from an outside wall. Be sure to keep far away from windows. The wind could smash them and send splinters of glass through the air.

If you are in school, follow directions. Your teacher will take you to a basement or to an inside hall. Crouch on your knees near an inner wall. Bend over and clasp your hands behind your head. Most important, keep away from glass windows.

If you are out in the country in a car, don't try to race the tornado. Get out, and find a ditch to lie in.

When there's a tornado, there is also thunder and lightning. So keep away from metal things and from anything that uses electricity. Lightning can travel along metal pipes, and also along electric and telephone wires.

Listen to a battery radio. The radio will tell you when the storm has passed by. Stay where you are safe until you are sure the tornado is over.

Tornadoes are scary. Even if you are not right in the funnel, there is heavy rain all around, dark skies, thunder, lightning, and lots of wind. Often there will be hailstones. They may be as big as golf balls, or even bigger.

Don't panic. Know what to do when there is a tornado. And know where to go.

There is no way to stop tornadoes. But you can be safe from them when you know what to do.

About the Author
Franklyn M. Branley

When Franklyn M. Branley started teaching long ago,
not many students your age studied science. Since
Mr. Branley was interested in science, he started teaching
it to his fourth-graders. Other teachers liked his ideas so
much that he wrote instructions on how to teach science.
Before long, he was writing science books for children too.

Mr. Branley believes that authors of nonfiction books
are like teachers. "They write so that readers will better
understand whatever the subject may be," he says. "Also,
the writer hopes the book has prodded the reader into
thinking and wondering."

You might enjoy reading some of Mr. Branley's books
about space. He has written several about our solar
system including *Floating in Space* and *The Planets in Our
Solar System, Stage 2.*

Reader Response

Open for Discussion

Think of a bad storm you have been in or one that someone has told you about. How was it like or unlike a tornado described in "Tornado Alert"? What was it like to be in it?

Comprehension Check

1. What is the author explaining with the diagram on page 188? Explain your answer.

2. Several real storms are described in "Tornado Alert." Choose one and make up a newspaper headline for it.

3. "Tornado Alert" describes places to go to be safer during a tornado. Why are most of them underground? Find facts in the selection to support your answer.

4. Find the word *waterspout* on page 186. Tell what **context clues** gave you the meaning of the word.

5. Find the word *crouch* on page 193. Tell what **context clues** gave you the meaning of the word.

Twister Tips Game

Play this game with a small group. One person is the twister who spins among the players, stops, and tags someone. The twister names a location from the selection such as in a car, at home, or at school. The tagged player then describes and acts out what safety steps to take when a tornado is coming. Each person in the group should get a turn being the twister.

Skill Lesson

Fact and Opinion

- A **statement of fact** can be proved true or false.

- A **statement of opinion** is what someone believes or thinks. There may or may not be a good reason to think this way.

- Words that express what someone feels or thinks are clues that a statement is an opinion. Look for clue words such as *believe, like,* and *should.*

Read "About Sharks" by Don C. Reed from *Boys' Life* magazine.

Talk About It

1. What is one statement of fact that you find in the article about sharks? Share your fact with a classmate.

2. What is one opinion about sharks that the author has? How do you know this is an opinion?

About SHARKS

by Don C. Reed

Sharks are as natural to the sea as sparrows are to the sky. They live in every neighborhood of the ocean, from warm tropic waters to the chilly depths. The Greenland shark lives among and beneath the Arctic Ice.

When I worked as a diver for an aquarium-zoo in California, I spent 11,000 hours underwater, often near sharks.

I like sharks. I believe they are worth saving. As predators, sharks help keep the

198

ocean healthy. They eat weak and sick fish, because those are the easiest to catch. This keeps fish disease from spreading, wiping out whole schools. In this way, sharks help other fish survive. Fish are a valuable source of food for humans and for livestock (fish meal is used to make cattle and chicken feed). Sharks protect our fish supply.

Sharks themselves make good eating for people, because they have no bones. (Their skeletons are made of cartilage, or gristle.) We can take a limited number of sharks for food without threatening them.

LOOK AHEAD TO

Danger—Icebergs!

In the next selection, you will discover many facts and a few opinions about icebergs. Watch for clue words to know which are statements of opinion.

Vocabulary

Words to Know

alert	ocean	thousands
breaks	melt	

Many words have more than one meaning. To decide which meaning is correct, look for clues in nearby sentences.

Read the ship's log. Pay special attention to its whole meaning. Decide whether *breaks* means "broken places" or "comes apart."

First Mate's Log

It's my job to look out for icebergs. I have to be <u>alert</u>, because icebergs could hurt our ship. An iceberg can be <u>thousands</u> of feet long before it <u>breaks</u> into smaller pieces. All icebergs <u>melt</u>, but melting can take a long time. If our ship hits one of the big icebergs, it could sink into the <u>ocean</u>. Everyone on the ship depends on me.

Write About It

An iceberg is floating in front of the ship. Tell what happens next. Use some of the vocabulary words.

DANGER– ICEBERGS!

by Roma Gans

Year after year, snow falls in the North. It falls on Alaska, Canada, Siberia, and Greenland. It also falls on the South Pole in Antarctica—where the penguins are.

Even the summer is cold in those places, so the snow does not melt. Over thousands of years it gets packed harder and harder until it is ice. In some places the ice can be three miles deep. This big cover of ice is called a glacier.

As the ice gets thicker and thicker in the glacier, it pushes toward the ocean.

The ocean waves beat hard against it. They make deep cracks in the glacier. All at once, there is a loud roar as a chunk of the glacier breaks off. This great chunk of ice is an iceberg.

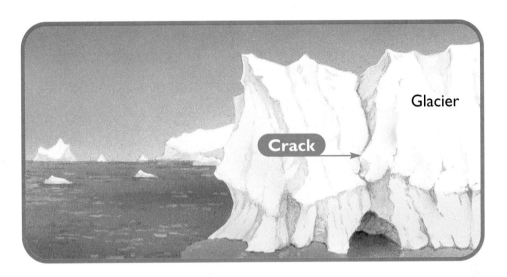

Thousands of icebergs break off from glaciers each year. Some are large and look like shiny mountains. Others look like big buildings. Some are very wide and flat. Entire towns could be built on them.

Bergs float away from the glacier slowly, moving only three or four miles per hour. You can walk faster than many bergs float. Ocean currents sweep them in and out of a straight line on their way to warmer waters. It may be three or four years before some bergs melt completely away.

Often, several bergs get pushed together and make an ice pack. The pack looks like a floating city of ice.

¹/₈ **Above Water**

Water Level

⁷/₈ **Below Water**

Sometimes an iceberg tilts to one side. It may even turn upside down. If it touches bottom, its high peaks will be scraped away. Sometimes little bergs may break off a big berg.

Sailors can see only the tops of bergs. About one-eighth of a berg floats above water, and about seven-eighths is hidden below. The part below stretches out deep and wide; it often has sharp edges. Ships stay far away to be safe, even from small bergs.

Holes are made in icebergs when the ice melts or is gashed out as a berg scrapes land. Seals and polar bears often crawl into these holes. Seal pups have been born in iceberg hollows. You can hear their yelps and barks.

Bubbles of air form in an iceberg, and when they break, anyone near hears a loud boom.

Hundreds of years ago there were brave sailors who crossed the Atlantic in wooden ships. They kept watch day and night. They had no telescopes or radios to guide them. They steered away from icebergs. Even when the sailors kept good watch, ships sometimes ran into icebergs and were sunk.

Even strong modern ships have struck bergs. One such crash happened in April 1912. A ship called the *Titanic* sailed from England on its first voyage. "Titanic" means large. The ship was the biggest and most beautiful ship ever built. No storms or icebergs could sink it—or so people said.

The *Titanic* leaves from England in 1912.

After four calm days of sailing, Captain E. J. Smith got radio messages that there were icebergs ahead. The ship sailed on.

Another radio alert came, but too late. There was a jerk and a grinding crash. The *Titanic* had hit an iceberg. Seams in the ship's metal hull began to give way.

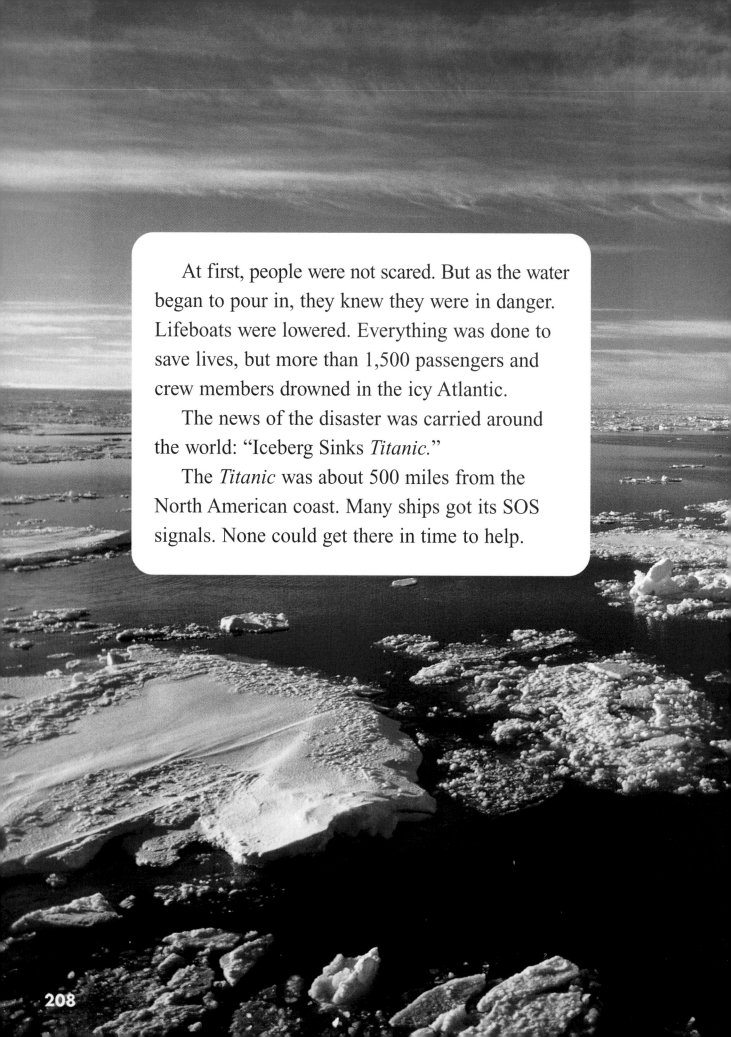

At first, people were not scared. But as the water began to pour in, they knew they were in danger. Lifeboats were lowered. Everything was done to save lives, but more than 1,500 passengers and crew members drowned in the icy Atlantic.

The news of the disaster was carried around the world: "Iceberg Sinks *Titanic*."

The *Titanic* was about 500 miles from the North American coast. Many ships got its SOS signals. None could get there in time to help.

Map shows the path of the *Titanic* and where it hit the iceberg and sank.

The berg that sank the *Titanic* was not large.
Survivors of the disaster said the berg's highest point
was about 100 feet above the water. Below water it
may have extended 500 feet down. It was almost
1,000 feet wide. The iceberg had broken off a glacier
in Greenland, on Baffin Bay. For three years it had
moved slowly south in the Atlantic with many much
larger bergs.

After the sinking of the *Titanic*, the berg drifted on.
As it moved into warmer waters, it began to melt. It
became filled with holes, and pieces broke off. It got
smaller and smaller. The last of the berg disappeared
months after the tragedy.

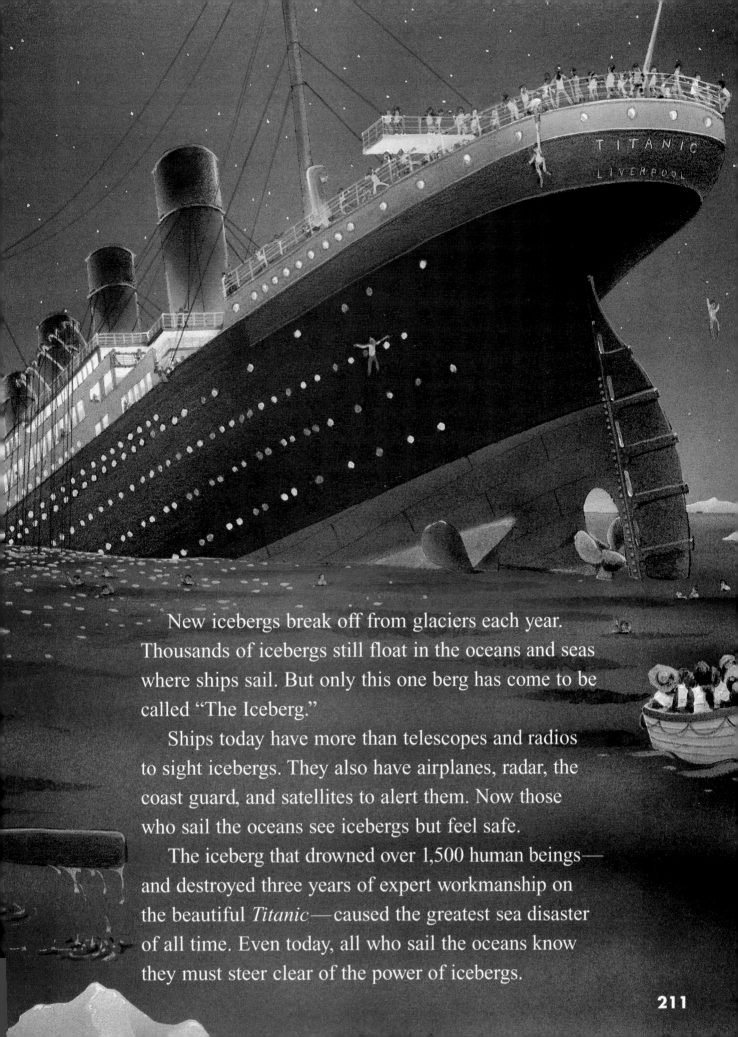

New icebergs break off from glaciers each year.
Thousands of icebergs still float in the oceans and seas
where ships sail. But only this one berg has come to be
called "The Iceberg."

Ships today have more than telescopes and radios
to sight icebergs. They also have airplanes, radar, the
coast guard, and satellites to alert them. Now those
who sail the oceans see icebergs but feel safe.

The iceberg that drowned over 1,500 human beings—
and destroyed three years of expert workmanship on
the beautiful *Titanic*—caused the greatest sea disaster
of all time. Even today, all who sail the oceans know
they must steer clear of the power of icebergs.

About the Author
Roma Gans

Roma Gans didn't start writing children's books until late in her life. Before she started writing, she was a teacher and a college professor. She wrote *Danger—Icebergs!* when she was eighty-two years old.

Something Ms. Gans enjoyed more than anything was watching children learn. As she wrote, she thought about the children who would read her books. "I write and visualize faces before me who are reading as I write," she said. She loved children!

Other books by Ms. Gans that you may enjoy include *How Do Birds Find Their Way?* and *Let's Go Rock Collecting*.

Reader Response

How do you think it would feel to be on a ship and see an iceberg? Explain.

Comprehension Check

1. The author tells about the size of icebergs in several ways. She uses numbers, adjectives, and comparisons. Which way gives you the best idea of the size of an iceberg? Explain.

2. One of the things that makes an iceberg dangerous is that it is much bigger than it looks. Why does an iceberg look smaller than it is?

3. Icebergs and tornadoes are both dangerous. Which one is more dangerous? Explain your answer.

4. Which sentence states a **fact,** and which states an **opinion?**

- The *Titanic* was the most beautiful ship ever built.
- When it was built, the *Titanic* was the biggest ship ever built.

5. Tell a **fact** about icebergs. Tell an **opinion** about them.

Cool Descriptions

Choose one of the iceberg pictures in the selection. Then write a few sentences describing it. Think about size, color, and shape. Give your description a title—"The Iceberg on Page ____."

Main Idea and Details

- The **main idea** is the most important idea of a paragraph. A main idea is sometimes stated in the paragraph.

- **Supporting details** are small pieces of information in the paragraph that tell more about the main idea.

Read "Shapes and Sizes of Sea Birds" from *Discovering Sea Birds* by Anthony Wharton.

Write About It

1. Work with a partner to write down the main idea of each paragraph. Use a separate sheet of paper for each main idea.

2. Decide what details support the main idea in each paragraph and write them under the main idea. Share your findings with other pairs.

Shapes and Sizes of Sea Birds

by Anthony Wharton

The bodies of many sea birds, such as albatrosses, penguins, and pelicans, are quite stoutly built. Others, like those of terns and petrels, are fairly slender. All of them, however, are very streamlined.

Sea birds vary a lot in size, which helps us to identify the different kinds. The smallest sea bird, a least storm petrel, is only about 13 cm (5 in.) in

puffin

gannet

cormorant

length. This is shorter than the bills of many albatrosses. The largest albatross has a wingspan of more than 360 cm (12 ft) and an emperor penguin may weigh as much as 40 kg (88 lb).

Sea birds' bills are very varied and can also help in identification. For example, most people can recognize a puffin because of its colorful, triangular bill. Pelicans, too, are easily recognized because of the shape of their pouched bills, which can hold up to 13.5 liters (3.5 gal) of water.

pelican

pacific gull   black-headed gull

LOOK AHEAD TO

Nights of the Pufflings

In the next selection, a little girl and her friends rescue baby puffins. Read and look for the details of how they do it.

Vocabulary

Words to Know

burrows	hatch	cliff
searching	cardboard	
underground	island	

Words that are pronounced the same but have different spellings and meanings are **homophones.** To understand the meaning of a homophone, look for clues near it.

Read this paragraph. Why is *burrows* used below and not *burros?*

Bird Rescue

We were on an island searching for birds hurt by an oil spill. Birds living up on the cliff were safe. Others tried to go underground. They made burrows in the sand on the shore. Their holes were filled with oil. We found a nest of eggs ready to hatch. We put them in a cardboard box to take them some place safe.

Write About It

Use vocabulary words in a slogan to get people to help rescue birds.

Nights
of the Pufflings

photographs and text by Bruce McMillan

Heimaey Island, Iceland, April

Halla searches the sky every day. As she watches from high on a cliff overlooking the sea, she spots her first puffin of the season. She whispers to herself, "Lundi," which means "puffin" in Icelandic.

Soon the sky is speckled with them—puffins, puffins everywhere. Millions of these birds are returning from their winter at sea. They are coming back to Halla's island and the nearby uninhabited islands to lay eggs and raise puffin chicks. It's the only time they come ashore.

While Halla and her friends are at school in the village beneath the cliffs, the puffins continue to land. These "clowns of the sea" return to the same burrows year after year. Once back, they busy themselves getting their underground nests ready. Halla and all the children of Heimaey can only wait and dream of the nights of the pufflings yet to come.

On the weekends, Halla and her friends climb over the cliffs to watch the birds. They see puffin pairs *tap-tap-tap* their beaks together. Each pair they see will soon tend an egg. Deep inside the cliffs that egg will hatch a chick. That chick will grow into a young puffling. That puffling will take its first flight. The nights of the pufflings will come.

In the summer, while Halla splashes in the cold ocean water, the puffins also splash. The sea below the cliffs is dotted with puffins bobbing on the waves. Like Halla, many puffins that ride the waves close to the shore are young. The older birds usually fly further out to sea where the fishing is better. The grown-up puffins have to catch lots of fish, because now that it's summer they are feeding more than just themselves.

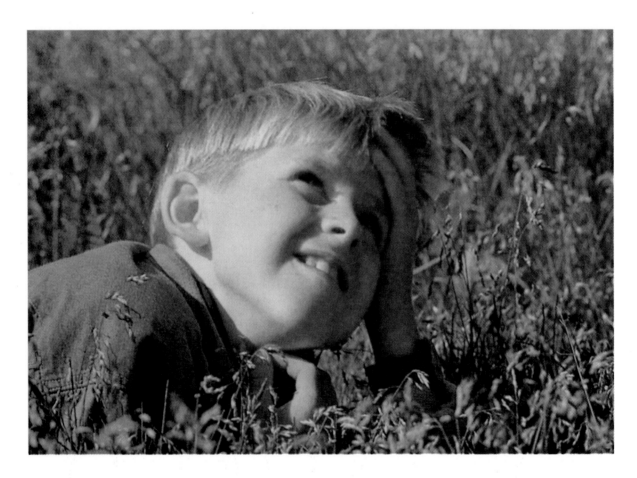

Halla's friend, Arnar Ingi, spies a puffin overhead. "Fisk," he whispers as he gazes at the returning puffin's bill full of fish. The puffin eggs have hatched, and the parents are bringing home fish to feed their chicks. The nights of the pufflings are still long weeks away, but Arnar Ingi thinks about getting some cardboard boxes ready.

Halla and her friends never see the chicks—only the chicks' parents see them. The baby puffins never come out. They stay safely hidden in the long dark tunnels of their burrows. But Halla and her friends hear them calling out for food. *"Peep-peep-peep."* The growing chicks are hungry. Their parents have to feed them—sometimes ten times a day—and carry many fish in their bills.

All summer long the adult puffins fish and tend to their feathers. By August, flowering baldusbrá blanket the burrows. With the baldusbrá in full bloom, Halla knows that the wait is over. The hidden chicks have grown into young pufflings. The pufflings are ready to fly and will at last venture out into the night. Now it's time.

It's time for Halla and her friends to get out their boxes and flashlights for the nights of the pufflings. Starting tonight, and for the next two weeks, the pufflings will be leaving for their winter at sea. Halla and her friends will spend each night searching for stranded pufflings that don't make it to the water. But the village cats and dogs will be searching too. It will be a race to see who finds the stray pufflings first. By ten o'clock the streets of Heimaey are alive with roaming children.

In the darkness of night, the pufflings leave their burrows for their first flight. It's a short, wing-flapping trip from the high cliffs. Most of the birds splash-land safely in the sea below. But some get confused by the village lights—perhaps they think the lights are moonbeams reflecting on the water. Hundreds of the pufflings crash-land in the village every night. Unable to take off from flat ground, they run around and try to hide. Dangers await. Even if the cats and dogs don't get them, the pufflings might get run over by cars or trucks.

Halla and her friends race to the rescue. Armed with their flashlights, they wander through the village. They search dark places. Halla yells out "puffling" in Icelandic. "Lundi pysja!" She has spotted one. When the puffling runs down the street, she races after it, grabs it, and nestles it in her arms. Arnar Ingi catches one, too. No sooner are the pufflings safe in the cardboard boxes than more of them land nearby. "Lundi pysja! Lundi pysja!"

For two weeks all the children of Heimaey sleep late in the day so they can stay out at night. They rescue thousands of pufflings. There are pufflings, pufflings, everywhere, and helping hands too—even though the pufflings instinctively nip at helping fingers. Every night Halla and her friends take the rescued pufflings home. The next day they send their guests on their way. Halla meets her friends and, with the boxes full of pufflings, they hike down to the beach.

It's time to set the pufflings free. Halla releases
one first. She holds it up so that it will get used to
flapping its wings. Then, with the puffling held
snugly in her hands, she counts "Einn-tveir-ÞRÍR!" as
she swings the puffling three times between her legs.
The last swing is the highest, launching the bird up in
the air and out over the water beyond the surf. It's only
the second time this puffling has flown, so it flutters
just a short distance before safely splash-landing.

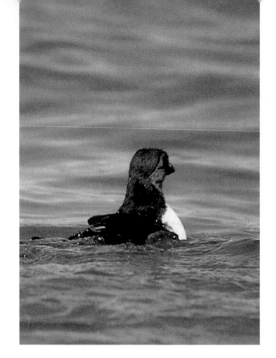

Day after day Halla's pufflings paddle away, until the nights of the pufflings are over for the year. As she watches the last of the pufflings and adult puffins leave for their winter at sea, Halla bids them farewell until next spring. She wishes them a safe journey as she calls out "good-bye, good-bye" in Icelandic. "Bless, bless!"

About the Author/Photographer

Bruce McMillan

Bruce McMillan's father gave him a camera when he was five, and he is still taking pictures. In high school, he couldn't afford his senior pictures, so he took pictures of himself to trade with friends. His pictures were different, though. "Using a top hat and some charcoal for a beard, I became Abe Lincoln," he remembers.

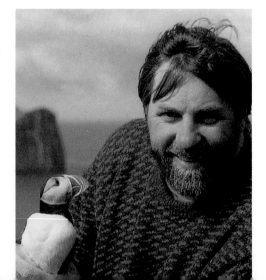

Open for Discussion

Would you like to take part in saving the pufflings? Why or why not?

Comprehension Check

1. Look at page 222. How does Arnar know that the pufflings have hatched?

2. How do Halla and her friends feel about the pufflings? Give examples from the selection to support your answer.

3. How could helping the pufflings be dangerous? When might it be unsafe to help some other animal in danger?

4. What is the **main idea** of the paragraph on page 227?

5. What **details support** that **main idea?**

Come to Iceland

Work with a partner to learn what Iceland looks like. Does it have mountains, lakes, big cities, trees, volcanoes? Make up a TV commercial to tell classmates what they'd see if they were tourists in Iceland.

Saving the Whooping Crane

by Faith McNulty

Reading Across Texts

Reading an Informational Article

✓ **Read the title.** This will tell you what the article is about. It is the topic.

✓ **Look for the main idea.** Paragraphs often tell a main idea. Each paragraph should be about the topic.

✓ **Read for details.** Details will tell you more about the main idea.

Focus Your Reading

This informational article tells you about how whooping cranes were saved from becoming extinct. As you read, think about how Halla and her friends saved the pufflings.

In the United States today you can see wild whooping cranes at their winter refuge on the Texas Coast, near the town of Aransas. Usually about fifty whooping cranes spend the winter there. In good years there are a few more; in bad years, less. They are the only wild whooping cranes left on earth. This is a very small number, and whooping cranes are on the list of species that might become extinct.

At the Aransas Refuge the whooping cranes do not stay in a flock, but spread out along the shore in family groups. A pair of cranes usually raises only one chick each season. If you visited the refuge you would probably see pairs with young cranes that were hatched in Canada the summer before. The young are a rusty pink color that changes to white as they grow up. During the winter the parent cranes feed their young one and also teach it to find its own food. In spring the cranes gather in small groups and take to the air, they circle higher and higher, then begin the long, long flight to their nesting place in Canada—twenty-two hundred miles away.

About thirty-five years ago conservationists—people who care about wildlife—realized that little by little whooping cranes were decreasing in number. Many cranes had been shot by hunters. Each year the cranes found fewer safe places to nest and raise their young. The wild shores and marshes where whooping cranes spent the winter were no longer wild and safe for them.

Year after year more cranes died than were hatched, or than lived to grow up and start new families. For some years no one noticed or cared that few whooping cranes could be seen where once there had been many. When people did notice—and care—it was almost too late to save the cranes. At this time, in the 1930s, there were only twenty or thirty whooping cranes left on earth. Unless they were protected quickly, there would soon be none at all.

It is lucky for the whooping cranes—and for all of us who love wildlife—that some people *did* care about the cranes. Our government's Fish and Wildlife Service bought the land at Aransas and turned it into a refuge— safe from hunters.

Clouds

by Aileen Fisher

Wonder where they come from?
Wonder where they go?
Wonder why they're sometimes high
and sometimes hanging low?
Wonder what they're made of,
and if they weigh a lot?
Wonder if the sky feels bare up there
    when clouds are *not?*

The Sky

by Lee Blair

It must be fun
to be the sky
and see an eagle
soaring high,
or hear and see
a gleaming jet
climb higher, higher,
higher yet.

But best of all,
the sky can trace
the route of rockets
out in space.
When eagles, jets
and rockets fly,
it must be fun
to be the sky.

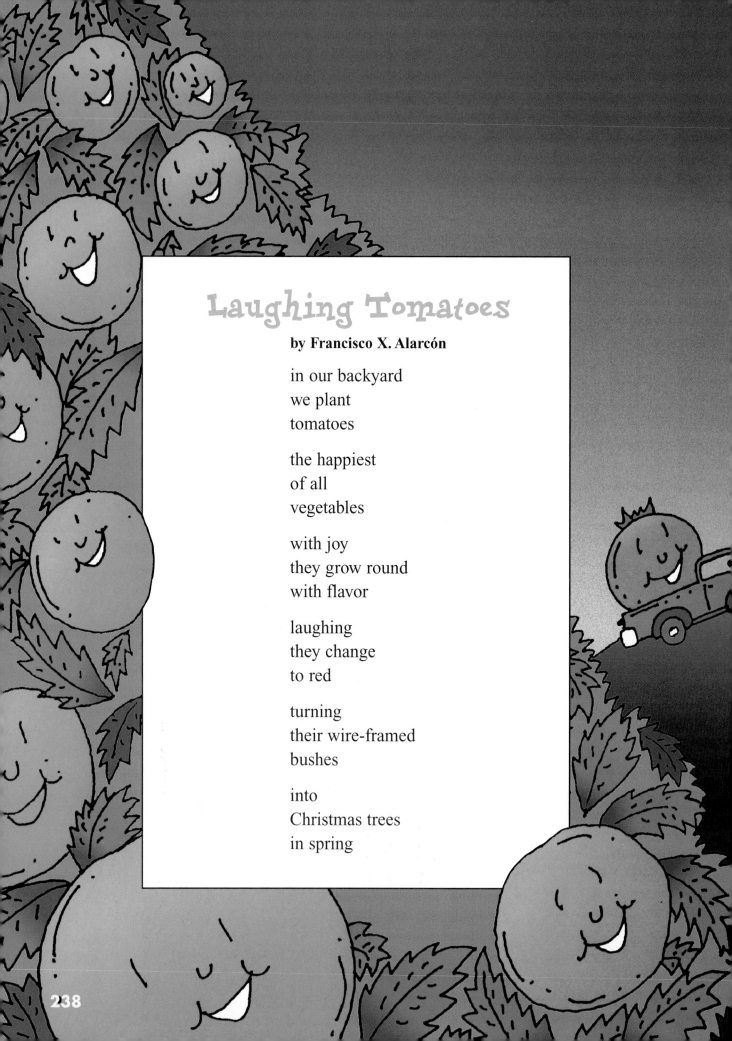

Laughing Tomatoes

by Francisco X. Alarcón

in our backyard
we plant
tomatoes

the happiest
of all
vegetables

with joy
they grow round
with flavor

laughing
they change
to red

turning
their wire-framed
bushes

into
Christmas trees
in spring

Fishes' Evening Song

by Dahlov Ipcar

Flip flop,
Flip flap,
Slip slap,
Lip lap;
Water sounds,
Soothing sounds.
We fan our fins
As we lie
Resting here
Eye to eye.
Water falls
Drop by drop,
Plip plop,

Drip drop,
Plink plunk,
Splash splish;
Fish fins fan,
Fish tails swish,
Swush, swash, swish.
This we wish . . .
Water cold,
Water clear,
Water smooth,
Just to soothe
Sleepy fish.

Getting the Job Done

How can we learn from everything we do?

Steps in a Process

- Following **steps in a process** usually means doing or making something.

- A process is a number of steps that follow in a certain order, from start to finish.

- Sometimes the steps in a process are shown in pictures as well as words.

Read "Cartoon Drawing" from *Cartooning for Kids* **by Carol Lea Benjamin.**

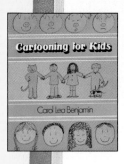

Write About It

1. Follow the steps given for drawing the pig. Share your drawing with a classmate.

2. Were the steps easy to follow? Why or why not?

Cartoon Drawing
by Carol Lea Benjamin

Get some paper and a pencil. You're going to begin by drawing a circle. Don't worry if the circle isn't perfectly round or if the beginning and the end of the circle don't meet. It doesn't matter. Don't jump ahead and try to copy the finished character. Even if the steps look easy to you, you're more likely to draw the character well if you go step by step.

1. Draw a circle.

2. Draw a smaller oval in the lower half of the circle.

3. Two little vertical lines in the oval become nostrils. Dots would work just as well.

4. Draw two small triangles for ears.

5. Two small vertical lines become eyes. Now your drawing will look like this.

6. Short horizontal lines look like eyebrows.

7. This character needs a mouth. It's just a small curve.

8. Hey! That's upside down.

9. Ah. Good work, cartoonist! Give your pig a name and . . .

10. Some lunch.

What Do Authors Do?

In the next selection, you will read about the steps an author takes to write a story.

Words to Know

**suggestions libraries museums
information difficult authors**

Many words have more than one meaning. To decide which meaning of a word is correct, look for clues in a nearby sentence or paragraph.

Read this paragraph. Pay special attention to its meaning as a whole. Decide whether *difficult* means "not easy to please" or "hard to do."

Writers' Work

Lee and Jae are authors who write children's books. It is difficult for them to write a book about Egypt because they don't know much about it. They need more information about mummies. They visit several libraries to find out more. One librarian gives them suggestions of books to read. Lee and Jae visit museums too. After looking at displays, they are ready to write.

Write About It

What is the best way to find information for a report? Use some vocabulary words to make a tip list.

What Do Authors Do?

written and illustrated by
Eileen Christelow

Authors get ideas for books at the strangest moments!

When authors have ideas for books, they start to write.

Sometimes it is difficult to find the words.

Some authors write notes about what might happen in the story. They make lists or outlines.

Some authors who write picture books are also illustrators. Sometimes they sketch as they write. The sketches give them ideas.

Sometimes authors need more information.

So they go to libraries, historical societies, museums. . . .

They read books, old newspapers, magazines, letters, and diaries written long ago. They take notes.

They interview people. They take more notes.

They listen and watch.

They write and write and write . . .

and cross things out . . .

throw parts of the story away . . . and start again.

Sometimes authors read their stories to their families.
Their families make suggestions.

Sometimes they read to author friends in a writers' group.
The friends make suggestions.

Sometimes authors get stuck, so they put their books away for a while.

But usually, when they are doing something else, they get unstuck.

Then they start to write again.

Authors who are also illustrators make
a dummy of the book to show how it will
look with illustrations.

It can take one year, two years, or more to finish
writing a manuscript! When the stories are finished,
authors send their manuscripts to publishers.

Sometimes they wait for weeks or months to hear
whether the publishers like their books.

Most authors have received rejection letters.
Some rejection letters are encouraging. Some are not.

But authors are very persistent people. They work on their manuscripts some more. They send their manuscripts out to other publishers.

Authors are very pleased when they find a publisher!

About the Author/Illustrator

Hi!
I'm Eileen Christelow.

Books have always been important to Eileen Christelow. Even before she could read, she loved them. "When I was about three or four, I dreamed I could read," she remembers, "turning page after page and reading all the words. But when I woke up, I could no longer read." When she did learn to read, she spent a lot of her time doing what she had dreamed.

Ms. Christelow got her love of books from her parents. Her father liked to read books about things such as economics and history, but he also loved comic books. Ms. Christelow and her brother were allowed to see the comic books only after their father finished them.

Later, when Ms. Christelow had a child of her own, they went to the library each week. Ms. Christelow began to think that maybe she could create a children's book. She found out that sometimes doing the writing and the illustrating is not as easy as it looks. Like the authors in *What Do Authors Do?*, it took her a long time to get her first picture book just right.

Open for Discussion

Both authors saw the same thing happen and got different story ideas. If you saw what they saw, what would your story be about? Why?

Comprehension Check

1. Why do you think Eileen Christelow tells about two authors in her story? Explain your answer.

2. In this selection what do the authors do when they are stuck? Which author has the better way of getting unstuck? Explain.

3. How do you think an author feels when a book is rejected? Why do you think so?

4. According to *What Do Authors Do?*, what is the very first **step in the process** of writing a book?

5. What is the **step in the process** that comes right after research?

Read My Book!

Create a book cover for the cat or dog book in *What Do Authors Do?* Make up a title for the cat or dog story. Include an author's and an illustrator's name. Draw a picture for the front cover, and write a few short sentences for the back cover that would make your friends want to read the book. Share your covers with classmates.

wacky man
by ron fridell

What do you need to be a good cartoonist?

- It helps to pay close attention to the world around you.

- It helps to have your own special way of looking at life—to be wacky.

- It helps to have a good sense of humor, of course.

It also helps to have lots of experiences. The more places you've been and the more things you've done, the better. Sean Higgins of San Antonio, Texas, had jobs as a librarian, construction worker, writer, chef, telephone operator, and parking attendant. His weekly newspaper cartoon, *Wacky Man,* shows an artist who has his own special way of looking at life.

Soap, water, and some elbow grease takes care of the odor.

But it only cuts straight lines.

Summarizing

- In a **summary** a few sentences tell the main ideas in a story or article.

- A summary of a story tells what the story is about without telling details.

Read "To Catch a Rabbit" from *The Blue Hill Meadows* by Cynthia Rylant.

The Blue Hill Meadows

Talk About It

1. Is *A* or *B* a better summary of the story?

A. Willie's mother enjoyed seeing wild rabbits. To surprise her, Willie planted a small garden to bring rabbits where his mother could see them.

B. On Mother's Day, Willie's mother saw him on the ground by her cherry tree. He was planting seeds and putting signs to mark the places.

2. What reasons do you have for your choice?

To Catch a Rabbit

by Cynthia Rylant

Wild rabbits are not easy to catch. They want to be free and they use their wits to stay that way. But Willie wasn't interested in catching the rabbit. His mother would not want a rabbit in a cage.

Willie was interested in making the rabbit stay, in making Eva's cherry tree the most wonderful place in the world for a rabbit to be.

And Willie thought he knew how to do it.

So, when Mother's Day morning came, Eva Meadow rose early from bed as usual, put on her robe, and quietly padded into the kitchen to

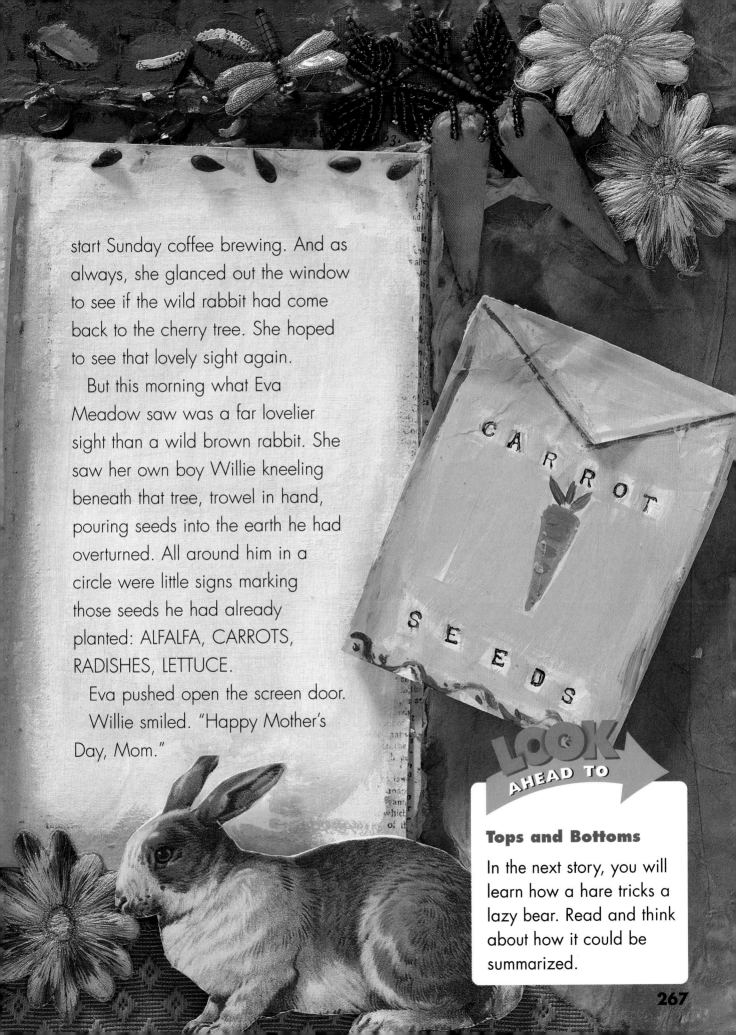

start Sunday coffee brewing. And as always, she glanced out the window to see if the wild rabbit had come back to the cherry tree. She hoped to see that lovely sight again.

But this morning what Eva Meadow saw was a far lovelier sight than a wild brown rabbit. She saw her own boy Willie kneeling beneath that tree, trowel in hand, pouring seeds into the earth he had overturned. All around him in a circle were little signs marking those seeds he had already planted: ALFALFA, CARROTS, RADISHES, LETTUCE.

Eva pushed open the screen door. Willie smiled. "Happy Mother's Day, Mom."

LOOK AHEAD TO

Tops and Bottoms

In the next story, you will learn how a hare tricks a lazy bear. Read and think about how it could be summarized.

Vocabulary

Words to Know

business   cheated partners
harvesting clever   wealth
lazy

Words with opposite meanings, like *up* and *down,* are **antonyms.** You can often figure out the meaning of a word by finding a clue near it. Sometimes this clue is an antonym.

Read this paragraph. Notice how the antonym *hardworking* helps you understand what *lazy* means.

The Lazy Cricket

Two crickets were <u>partners</u>. They had a <u>business</u> together <u>harvesting</u> wheat. One cricket was hardworking. The other was <u>lazy</u> but <u>clever</u>. Every night, the crickets piled up the wheat they had harvested. The lazy cricket <u>cheated</u> his partner out of his <u>wealth</u> by switching piles of wheat. One day . . .

Talk About It

Finish the story. Tell how the lazy cricket learns a lesson. Use some vocabulary words.

Tops
and Bottoms

adapted and illustrated
by Janet Stevens

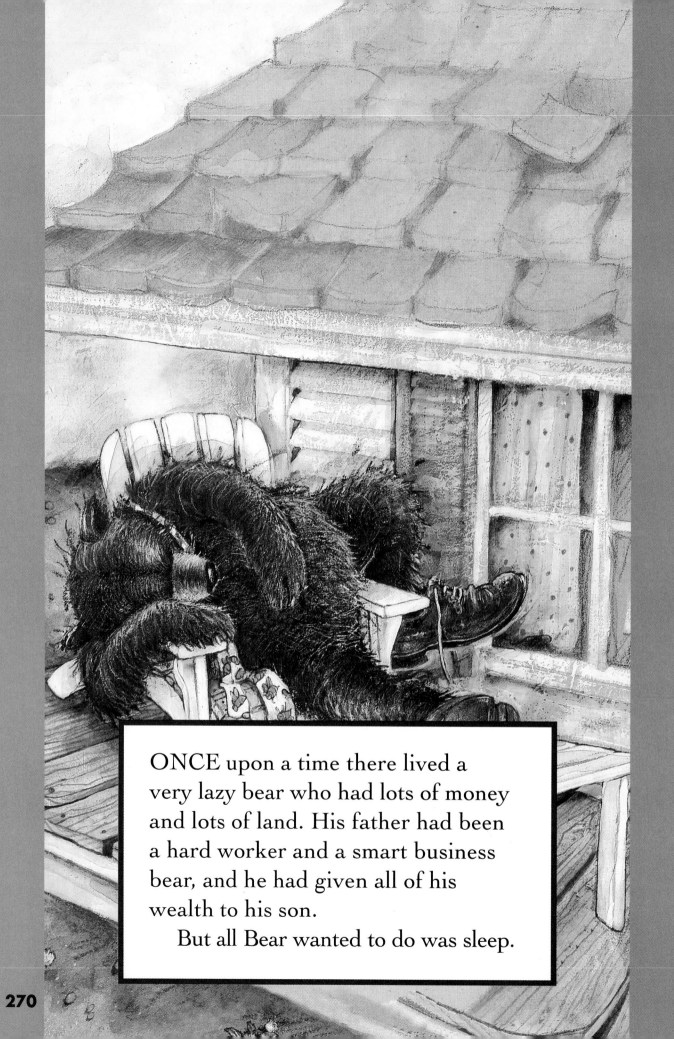

ONCE upon a time there lived a
very lazy bear who had lots of money
and lots of land. His father had been
a hard worker and a smart business
bear, and he had given all of his
wealth to his son.

But all Bear wanted to do was sleep.

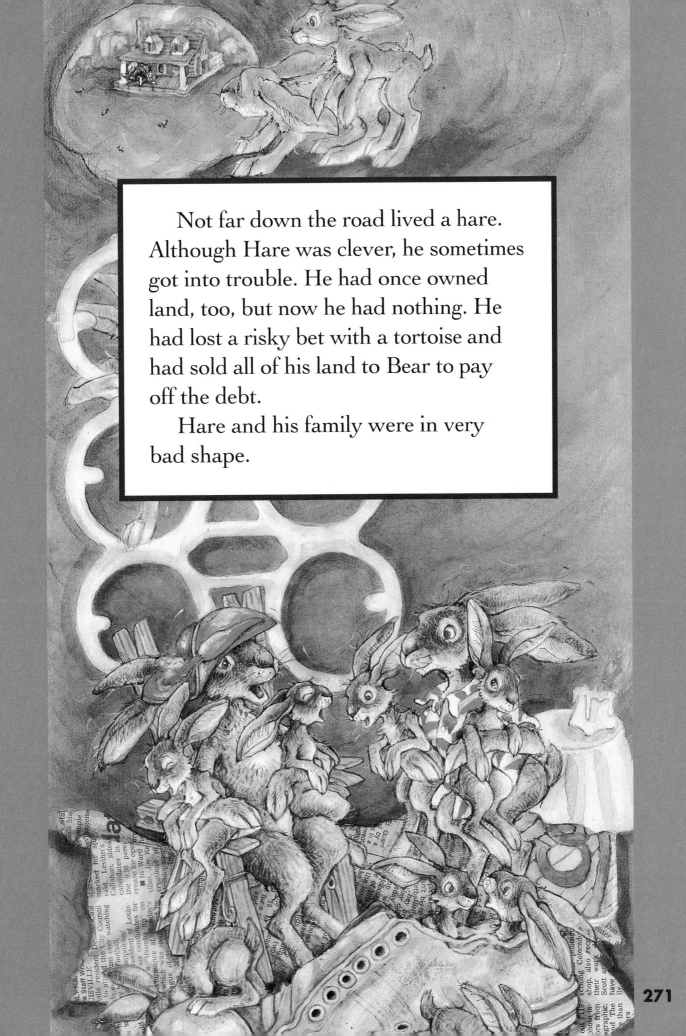

Not far down the road lived a hare. Although Hare was clever, he sometimes got into trouble. He had once owned land, too, but now he had nothing. He had lost a risky bet with a tortoise and had sold all of his land to Bear to pay off the debt.

Hare and his family were in very bad shape.

"The children are so hungry, Father Hare!
We must think of something!" Mrs. Hare cried
one day. So Hare and Mrs. Hare put their
heads together and cooked up a plan.

The next day Hare hopped down the road
to Bear's house. Bear, of course, was asleep.

"Hello, Bear, wake up! It's your neighbor,
Hare, and I have an idea!"

Bear opened one eye and grunted.

"We can be business partners!" Hare said. "All we need is this field right here in front of your house. I'll do the hard work of planting and harvesting, and we can split the profit down the middle. Yes, sir, Bear, we're in this together. I'll work and you sleep."

"Huh?" said Bear.

"So, what will it be, Bear?" asked Hare. "The top half or the bottom half? It's up to you—tops or bottoms?"

"Uh, let's see," Bear said with a yawn. "I'll take the top half, Hare. Right — tops."

Hare smiled. "It's a done deal, Bear."

So Bear went back to sleep, and Hare and his family went to work. Hare planted, Mrs. Hare watered, and everyone weeded.

Bear slept as the crops grew.

When it was time for the harvest, Hare called out, "Wake up, Bear! You get the tops and I get the bottoms."

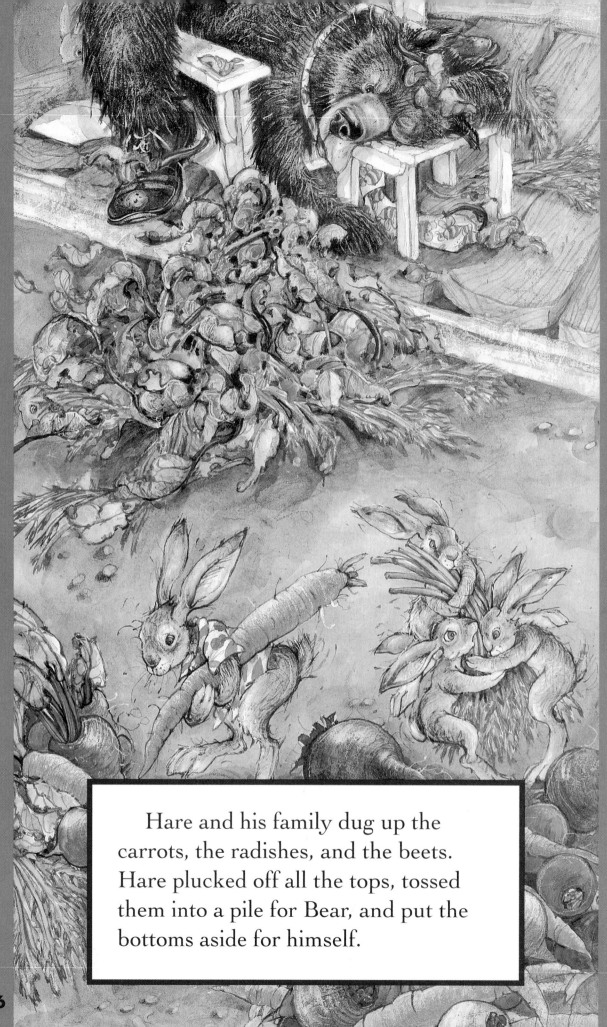

Hare and his family dug up the carrots, the radishes, and the beets. Hare plucked off all the tops, tossed them into a pile for Bear, and put the bottoms aside for himself.

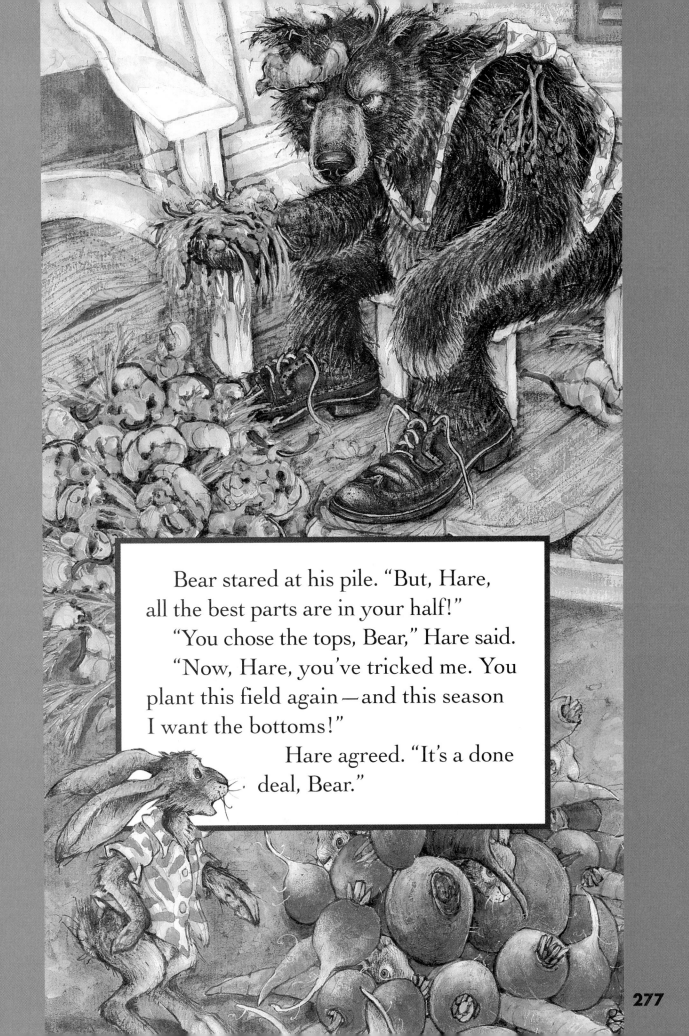

Bear stared at his pile. "But, Hare, all the best parts are in your half!"

"You chose the tops, Bear," Hare said.

"Now, Hare, you've tricked me. You plant this field again—and this season I want the bottoms!"

Hare agreed. "It's a done deal, Bear."

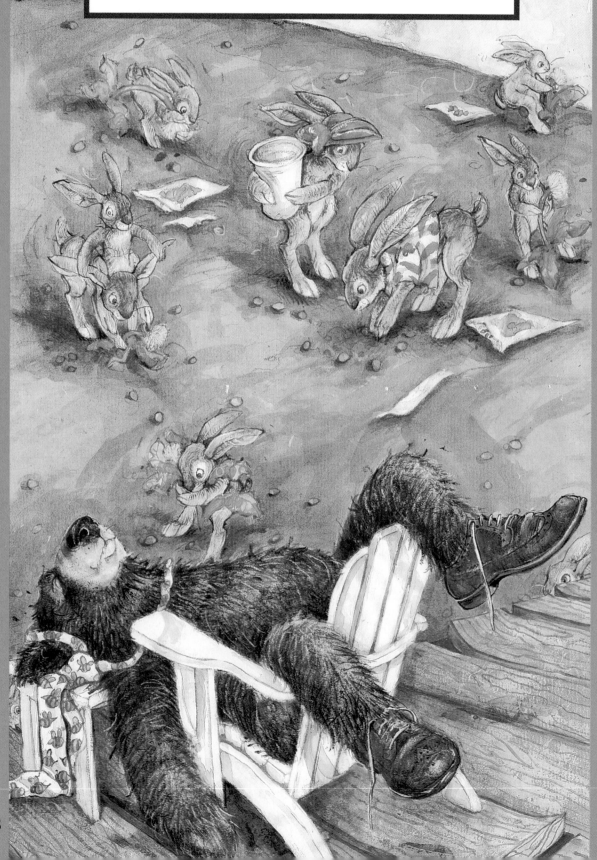

So Bear went back to sleep, and
Hare and his family went to work.
They planted, watered, and weeded.

Bear slept as the crops grew.

When it was time for the harvest, Hare called out, "Wake up, Bear! You get the bottoms and I get the tops."

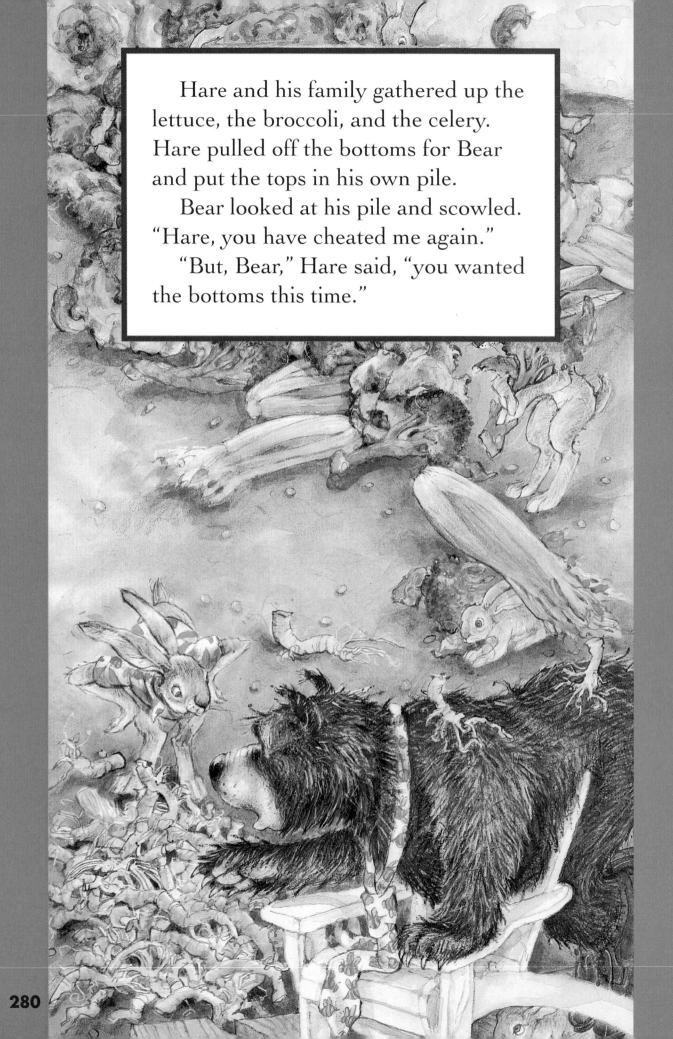

Hare and his family gathered up the lettuce, the broccoli, and the celery. Hare pulled off the bottoms for Bear and put the tops in his own pile.

Bear looked at his pile and scowled. "Hare, you have cheated me again."

"But, Bear," Hare said, "you wanted the bottoms this time."

Bear growled. "You plant this field again, Hare. You've tricked me twice, and you owe me one season of both tops and bottoms!"

"You're right, poor old Bear," sighed Hare. "It's only fair that you get both tops and bottoms this time. It's a done deal, Bear."

So Bear went back to sleep, and Hare and his family went to work. They planted, watered, and weeded, then watered and weeded some more.

Bear slept as the crops grew.

When it was time for the harvest, Hare called out, "Wake up, Bear! This time you get the tops and the bottoms!"

There in front of Bear's house lay a high field of corn. Hare and his family yanked up every cornstalk. Hare tugged off the roots at the bottom and the tassels at the top and put them in a pile for Bear. Then he carefully collected the ears of corn in the middle and placed them in his own pile.

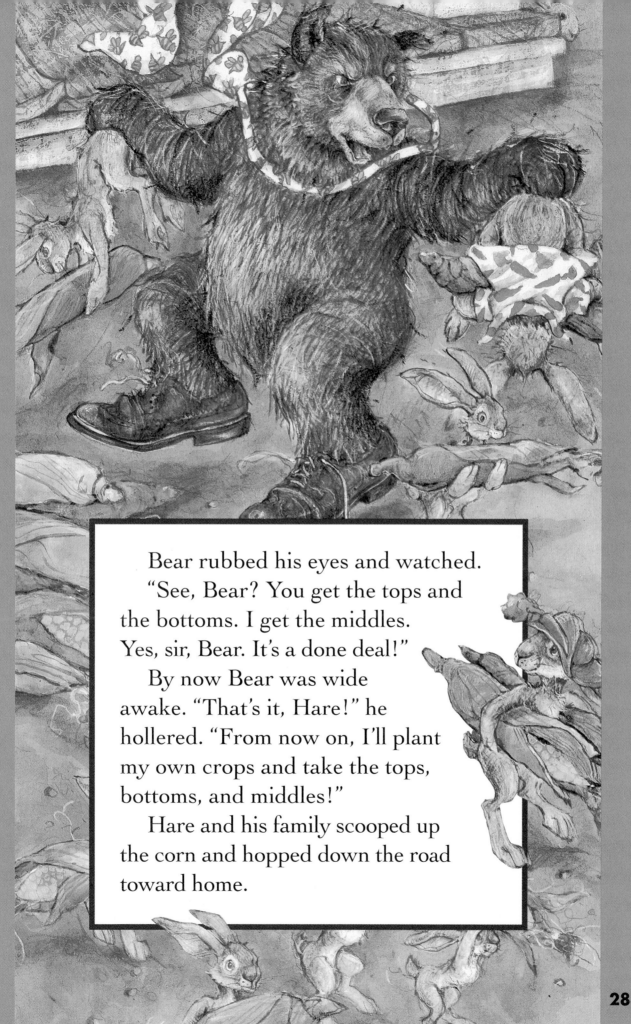

Bear rubbed his eyes and watched. "See, Bear? You get the tops and the bottoms. I get the middles. Yes, sir, Bear. It's a done deal!"

By now Bear was wide awake. "That's it, Hare!" he hollered. "From now on, I'll plant my own crops and take the tops, bottoms, and middles!"

Hare and his family scooped up the corn and hopped down the road toward home.

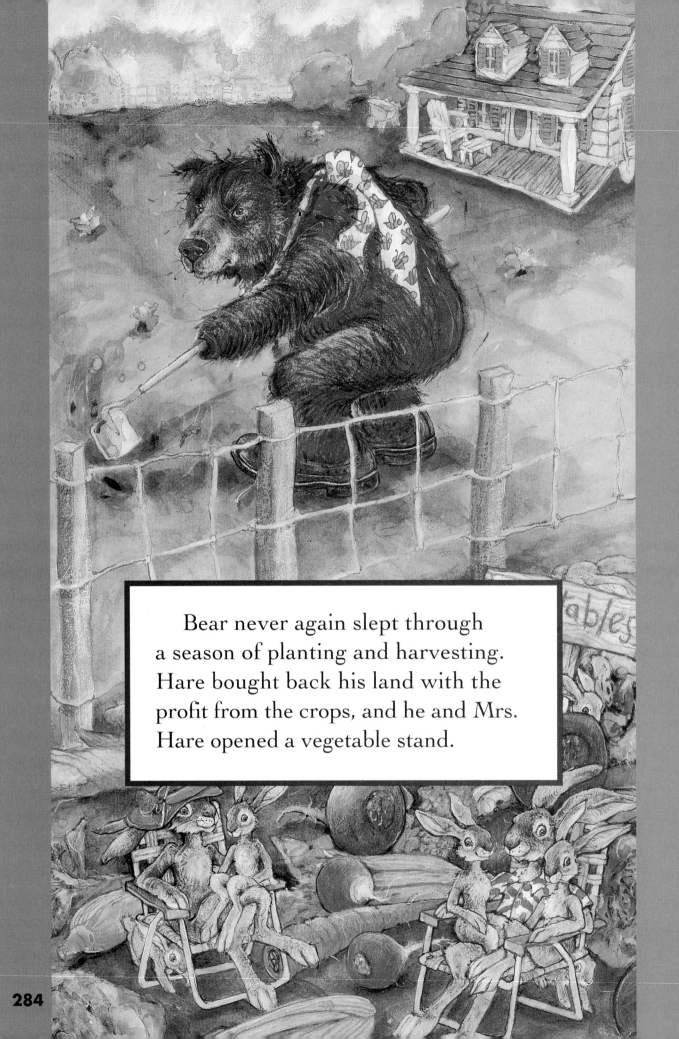

Bear never again slept through
a season of planting and harvesting.
Hare bought back his land with the
profit from the crops, and he and Mrs.
Hare opened a vegetable stand.

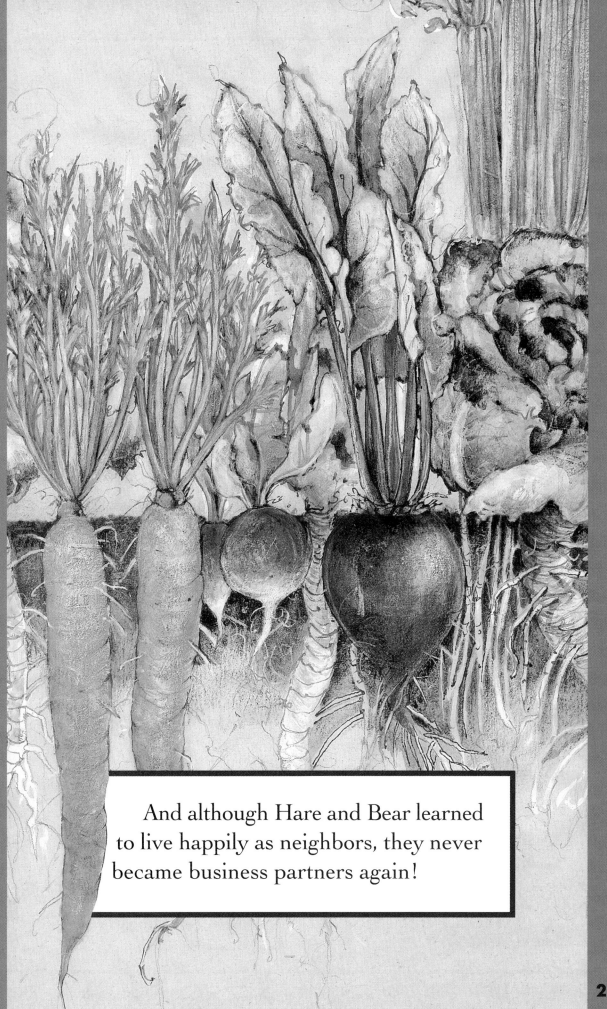

And although Hare and Bear learned to live happily as neighbors, they never became business partners again!

Janet Stevens

I was poking around in the library one day, looking for book ideas, but I wasn't having much luck on my own. Judy Volc, the children's librarian, seems to know everything about what kids like to read, so I asked her, "Do you have any suggestions? What stories do kids like?" She immediately replied, "*Tops and Bottoms!* Kids love that story—they ask for it over and over, and you could make it into a super picture book."

So began the *Tops and Bottoms* adventure. The librarian gave me several versions of the story, and I set out to retell it in my own words. But those words didn't come easily. The more I tried, the worse it sounded. So I put the words away. I thought, "I'll just draw! I'll have some fun." And so I began drawing *Tops and Bottoms* without a written story of my own.

Most of the versions the librarian gave me had people as the main characters. I like to draw animals, so I decided to make the lazy character a bear. But who should be his partner? First I tried a bear with a prairie dog.

Then I tried a bear with a fox. That wasn't right either. Then I changed the bear to a turtle. That switch reminded me of my illustrations of *The Hare and the Tortoise,* in which the hare loses the race. A loss like that could be the reason that Hare doesn't have any money! So I returned to my first idea of Bear, and his business partner became Hare! Sometimes you have to try lots of ideas before you get one that feels just right.

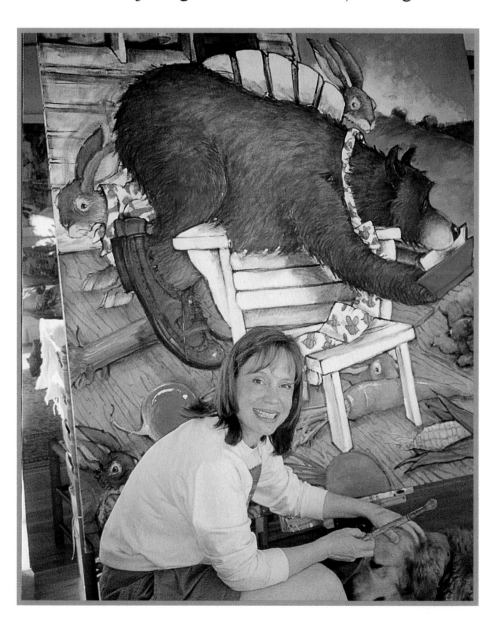

One of the most puzzling things to me about *Tops and Bottoms* is how I convinced myself I couldn't write the story. We really can talk ourselves into—or out of—things. It's sort of like *The Little Engine That Could;* the little train doesn't say, "I think I can't, I think I can't!" Drawing pictures first of Bear and Hare helped me get to know them. As I dressed them up and knew their personalities, they started to talk. Then I could write the story. The more I drew them the more confident I became. The words flowed easily once I quit worrying about whether I could write. That's why I dedicated the book to Judy Volc, the children's librarian; she thought I could create a *Tops and Bottoms* picture book from the beginning. All I needed to do was convince myself!

Open for Discussion

How do the pictures help tell the story? Tell which picture is your favorite, and why.

Comprehension Check

1. Does Hare treat Bear fairly? Why do you think this?

2. Tell one or two words that describe Hare's character.

3. Make a chart that lists vegetables in the story by the part that we eat—tops, bottoms, or middles. Add other vegetables that you eat.

4. To make a **summary** of the story, answer these questions.
   • What does Hare want?
   • How does he try to get it?
   • Does Hare get what he wants?

5. To make a different **summary** of the story, answer these questions.
   • What does Bear want?
   • How does he try to get it?
   • Does Bear get what he wants?

Hare Stories

Tell a partner another story about a hare, such as "The Tortoise and the Hare," or make up your own story. Discuss how the hares in the stories you tell are like the hare in *Tops and Bottoms*.

Text Structure

- **Text structure** is the way a story or article is organized.

- One way an author can organize the text is to tell things in the order that they happen.

- Use what you already know about story order to understand what you are reading.

Read "Puppy Training" from *Puppy Training and Critters, Too!* **by Judy Petersen-Fleming and Bill Fleming.**

Talk About It

1. How is this article organized?

2. What events happen once the puppy is used to wearing the collar?

Puppy Training

by Judy Petersen-Fleming
and Bill Fleming

Before you start training your puppy to walk on a leash, she should already be comfortable wearing a collar. Once she's used to her collar, you can make wearing a leash comfortable and positive. Start by putting on the leash and holding the other end so that it's loose. *Never* hold the leash tight so that you're pulling on your puppy. Run around and play with your puppy until she feels comfortable wearing the leash.

Now that your puppy is content *wearing* a leash, it is time to teach her to *walk* on a leash. It is important to teach this to your puppy so that she will be able to accompany you away from home. Start by holding the end of the leash with your right hand and the middle of the leash with your left hand. Your puppy should *always* be on your left side. Start walking slowly with your puppy next to you. If she stops, say "Heel" and tug gently on the leash. This will teach your puppy to walk beside you. Remember to keep these sessions short. Make walking on a leash fun for your puppy by taking her to new places each time.

LOOK AHEAD TO

Mom's Best Friend

In the next selection, you will read about a woman and her new dog. As you read, think about how the selection is organized.

Vocabulary

Words to Know

bounded	easily	introduce
correcting	guide	patient
direction	harness	

Words that are pronounced and spelled the same but have different meanings are called **homonyms.** *Bark* (on a tree) and *bark* (like a dog) are homonyms. To know the meaning being used, look for clues in the sentences near it.

Read this paragraph. Decide if the homonym *bounded* means "limited" or "jumped."

Harley Comes Home

The trainer came to introduce me to Harley, my new dog. Harley bounded in, excited to be home. I learned to hold his harness. Harley would guide me in the right direction. He easily helped me around the house, but he needed correcting when we went outside. I'll be patient—Harley will learn soon enough!

Write About It

Use vocabulary words to write ways that animals help people.

292

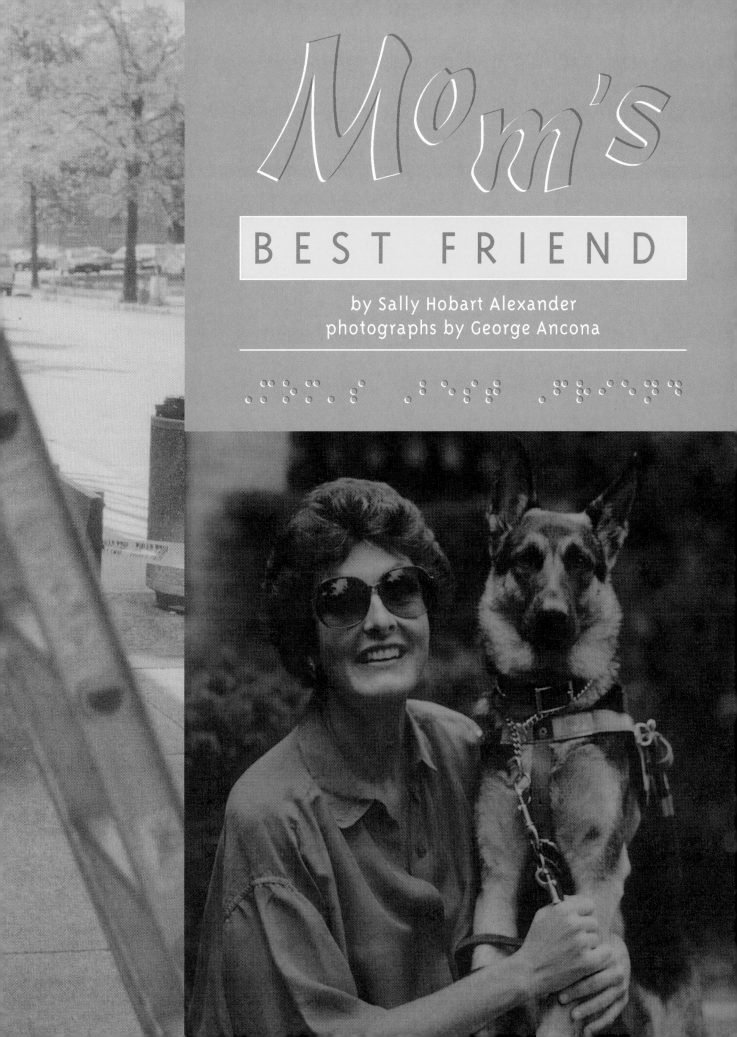

Mom's

BEST FRIEND

by Sally Hobart Alexander
photographs by George Ancona

The whole family loved Marit, Mom's dog guide. But when Marit dies, Mom has to go away to Seeing Eye, a school where new dog guides and their owners are trained. Leslie, Joel, and Dad are having trouble taking care of things without Mom.

Dear Mom,

Come home soon. The house misses you.

Love,

Exhausted in Pittsburgh

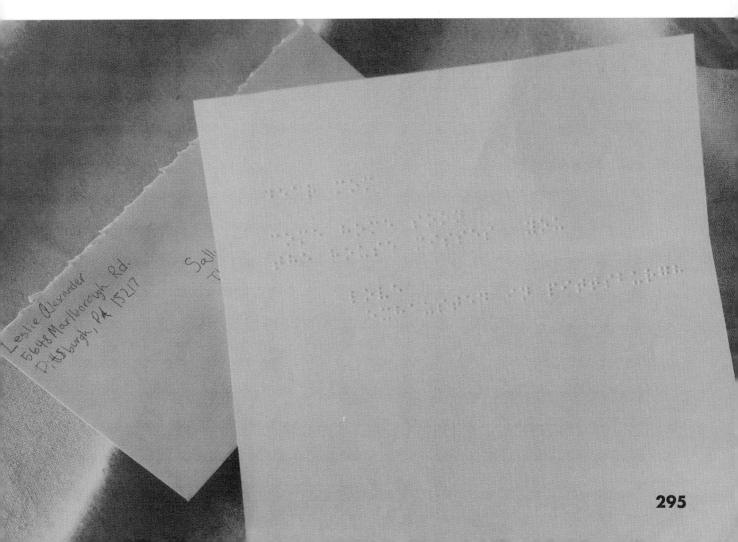

Mom wrote back.

Dear Exhausted,

Hang on. We'll be home to "hound" you Thursday. Be prepared. When you see me, I will have grown four more feet.

Mom

I couldn't laugh. I was too tired and worried. What if I couldn't love Ursula? Marit was the best dog ever.

Soon they arrived. Ursula yanked at her leash and sprang up on me. She pawed my shoulders, stomach, and arms just the way Marit used to, nearly knocking me over. She leaped onto Joel, licking him all over. As she bounded up onto me again, I realized Mom was right. Like magic, I was crazy about this shrimpy new dog.

But by the end of the day, I had a new worry. Was *Ursula* going to love *me?* She seemed friendly enough, but keyed up, even lost in our house.

"Remember how Marit loved you, Leslie? When you were little, she let you stand on her back to see out the window. Ursula will be just nuts about you. Love is the whole reason this dog guide business works."

So I tried to be patient and watched Mom work hard. First she showed one route in our neighborhood to Ursula and walked it over and over. Then she taught her a new route, repeated that, and reviewed the old one. Every day she took Ursula on two trips, walking two or three miles. She fed her, groomed her, gave her obedience training. Twice a week Mom cleaned Ursula's ears and brushed her teeth.

"I'm as busy as I was when you and Joel were little!" she said.

Mom and Ursula played for forty-five minutes each day. Joel, Dad, and I were only allowed to watch. Ursula needed to form her biggest attachment to Mom.

Mom made Ursula her shadow. When she showered or slept, Ursula was right there.

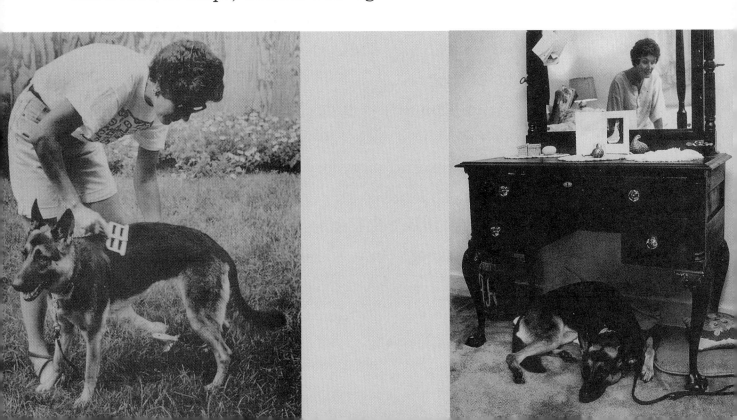

Still, Ursula didn't eat well—only half the amount she'd been eating at Seeing Eye. And she tested Mom, pulling her into branches, stepping off curbs. Once she tried to take a shortcut home. Another time, because she was nervous, she crossed a new street diagonally.

Crossing streets is tricky. Ursula doesn't know when the light is green. Mom knows. If she hears the cars moving beside her in the direction in which she's walking, the light is green. If they're moving right and left in front of her, it's red.

Mom said it takes four to six months for the dogs to settle down. But no matter how long she and Ursula are teamed up together, Ursula will need some correcting. For instance, Ursula might act so cute that a passerby will reach out to pet her. Then Mom will have to scold Ursula and ask the person not to pet a dog guide. If people give Ursula attention while she's working, she forgets to do her job.

After a month at home, Ursula emptied her food bowl every time. She knew all the routes, and Mom could zip around as easily as she had with Marit.

"Now it's time to start the loneliness training," Mom said. She left Ursula alone in the house, at first for a short time while she went jogging with Dad. Ursula will never be able to take Mom jogging because she can't guide at high speeds.

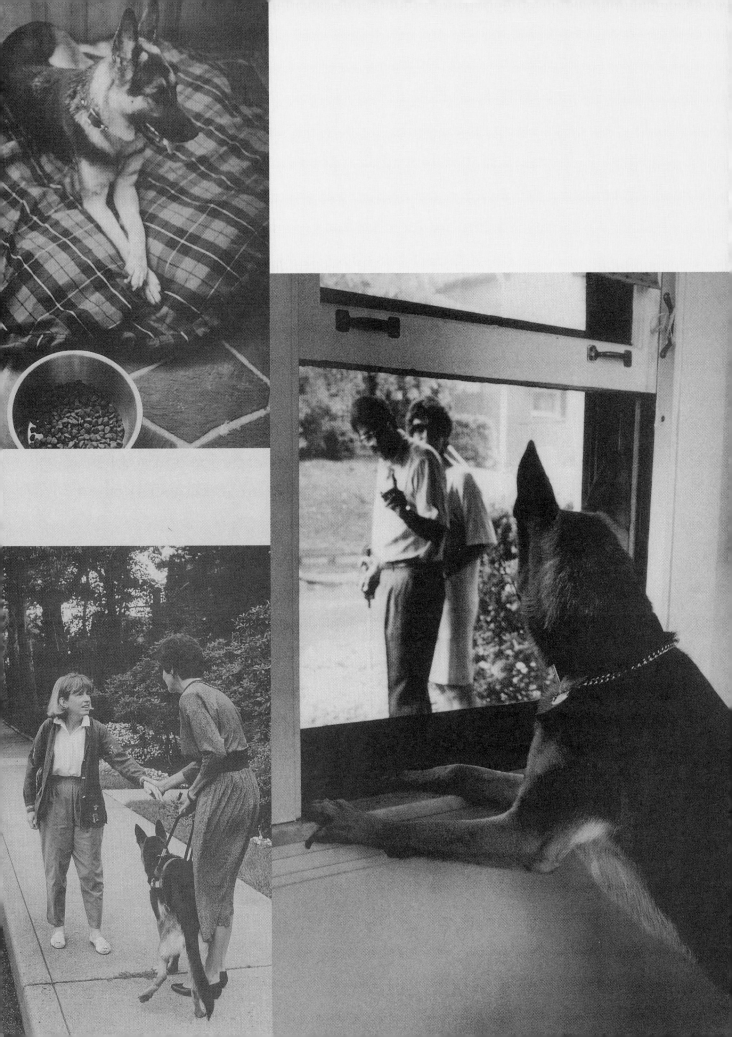

Each week Mom increased the amount of time Ursula was alone. I felt sorry for our pooch, but she did well: no barking, no chewing on furniture.

Then Mom said Joel and I could introduce Ursula to our friends, one at a time. They could pet her when she was out of harness.

Every morning Ursula woke Joel and me. Every night she sneaked into my bed for a snooze.

Finally Mom allowed Joel and me to play with Ursula, and I knew: shrimpy little Ursula had fallen for us, and we were even crazier about her.

But we haven't forgotten Marit. Joel says that Ursula is the best dog alive. And I always say she's the best dog in this world.

About the Author

When it comes to writing stories, Sally Hobart Alexander would like everyone to know this: "If I can do it, you can too!" Ms. Alexander started telling stories to her first child. By the time her second child came along, she could invent a story within seconds, using whatever characters her children suggested.

Ms. Alexander's stories for her children were make believe. Her book *Mom's Best Friend* and an earlier story, *Mom Can't See Me,* are based on her real-life experiences with blindness.

Sally Hobart Alexander

George Ancona

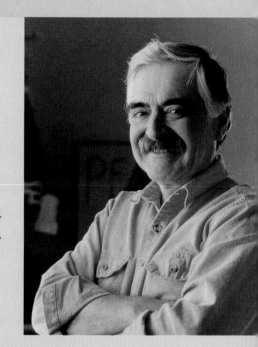

About the Photographer

When he was young, George Ancona's father took him to see huge ships on the waterfront in Brooklyn, New York. "It's like seeing something awe-inspiring and you just have to say, 'WOW'," he remembers. He thinks about that feeling as he creates his books.

Mr. Ancona has taken photographs for books written by other people as well as for his own books. For each book he took the pictures first. "The words came later," he says. "They filled in what the pictures couldn't convey."

Open for Discussion

Why is a dog Mom's best friend? When might an animal be your best friend?

Comprehension Check

1. In her replies to Leslie's letter, Mom makes two funny word jokes. Explain one of them.

2. Why is a dog guide's training so important?

3. Why is Leslie worried about being able to love Ursula?

4. *Mom's Best Friend* is nonfiction, but its **text structure** is like a story. How are most stories told?

5. Think about the **text structure** of this selection. What important event happened before the selection began?

Braille Bulletin Board

Use an encyclopedia or other books to find facts about Braille and how it is used. On an index card, write your fact about Braille. The class can collect and arrange the facts on a bulletin board.

Visualizing

- To **visualize** is to create a picture in your mind.

- You can put yourself into the story or article by using all your senses when you read.

- When you read, use details in the text along with what you know about the subject to see, hear, smell, taste, and feel what the author describes.

Read "A Ride to the Stars" from *A Net of Stars* by Jennifer Richard Jacobson.

Write About It

1. What details in the first two paragraphs help you visualize the midway?

2. What details in the third and fourth paragraphs help you visualize what Etta sees, hears, and feels on the Ferris wheel?

A Ride to the Stars

by Jennifer Richard Jacobson

We always go back to the midway on the last night. Now the midway looks like a fairyland with rainbow lights. The carnival music sounds louder than the roller coaster screams.

"Stay together," says Daddy. Fiona and Harper pay fifty cents to try and win a prize.

I don't say anything. I run over to the woman in the booth and buy the right number of tickets. The ticket man takes my tickets and snaps the bar across my lap. I close my eyes tight tight, and feel the chair go up. I know I'm getting higher. I know I'm in the sky. When

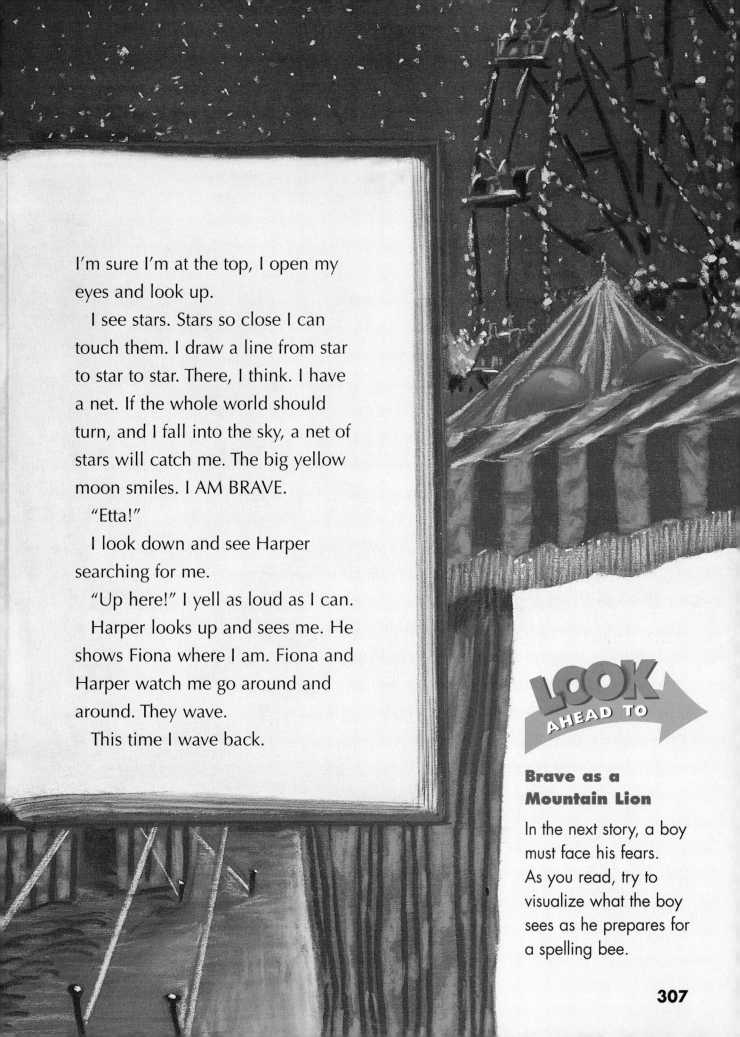

I'm sure I'm at the top, I open my eyes and look up.

I see stars. Stars so close I can touch them. I draw a line from star to star to star. There, I think. I have a net. If the whole world should turn, and I fall into the sky, a net of stars will catch me. The big yellow moon smiles. I AM BRAVE.

"Etta!"

I look down and see Harper searching for me.

"Up here!" I yell as loud as I can.

Harper looks up and sees me. He shows Fiona where I am. Fiona and Harper watch me go around and around. They wave.

This time I wave back.

LOOK AHEAD TO

Brave as a Mountain Lion

In the next story, a boy must face his fears. As you read, try to visualize what the boy sees as he prepares for a spelling bee.

Words to Know

spelling trouble   brave
afraid   reservation silent

As you read, you may come across a word you don't know. To figure out its meaning, look for clues in the words and sentences around it. An explanation given before or after the unknown word may contain a clue to its meaning.

Notice how *reservation* is used in the paragraph below. Find an explanation near it.

Facing the Challenge

Elena was in trouble. She was proud to be in the spelling contest, but she was afraid too. She had never left the reservation, the land on which her people lived. On the long bus ride, Elena was silent. She spelled words out in her head. The bus pulled up, and Elena suddenly felt brave. She finally knew she was ready.

Write About It

Describe a time when you did something difficult. Use some vocabulary words.

Brave as a Mountain Lion

by Ann Herbert Scott
illustrated by Glo Coalson

It was snowing hard. Pressing his face against the cold glass of the living room window, Spider could barely see his father's horses crowding against the fence. Soon the reservation would be covered with darkness.

Spider shivered. Any other night he would have been hoping his father would reach home before the snow drifted too high to push through. But tonight was different. Tonight he dreaded his father's coming.

In his pocket Spider could feel two pieces of paper from school. One he wanted to show his father. One he didn't. Not tonight. Not ever.

Beside him on the couch his sister Winona was playing with her doll. Lucky kid, thought Spider. Winona was too little to worry about anything, especially school.

Just then Spider saw the blinking red lights of the snowplow clearing the road beside their house. Right behind came his father's new blue pickup. Spider sighed. At least Dad was home safe. Now the trouble would begin!

Winona ran to the back door. But Spider stayed on the couch, waiting. From the kitchen he could smell dinner cooking. His favorite, deer meat. But tonight he didn't even feel like eating. Soon he heard the sound of his father and his brother Will stomping the snow from their boots.

Spider's father came in with an armful of mail from the post office. He hung up his hat and jacket on the pegs by the kitchen and stretched out in his favorite chair.

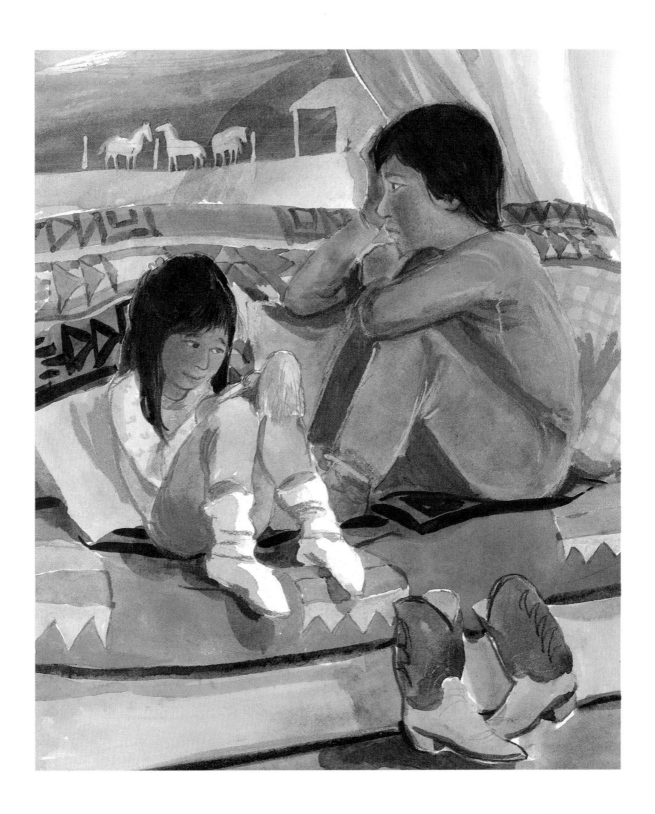

"So what did you do in school today?" he asked Spider.

"Not much," said Spider, feeling his pocket.

"Did you bring home any papers?"

Spider nodded. How did his father always know?

"Let's take a look," said his father.

Spider took the first paper from his pocket. "Here's the good one," he said.

"Spelling one hundred percent. Every word correct. Good for you, son."

"But, Dad, I'm in trouble." Spider shoved the other paper into his father's hand. "The teacher wants me to be in the big school spelling bee."

Spider's father read out loud: "Dear Parent, I am pleased to inform you that your son Spider has qualified for the school spelling bee, which will be held next Thursday night. We hope you and your family will attend."

Spider's mother and grandmother came in from the kitchen with the platter of deer meat and bowls of beans and corn for dinner. "That's a good report, Little Brother," his grandmother said, smiling.

"But I won't do it," said Spider.

"Why not?" asked Will.

"I'm too afraid," said Spider.

"But you're a brave boy," said his father. "Why are you afraid?"

"Dad," said Spider, "you have to stand high up on the stage in the gym and all the people look at you. I'm afraid my legs would freeze together and I wouldn't be able to walk. And if I did get up there, no sound would come out when I opened my mouth. It's too scary."

"Oh, I see," said his father.

Spider's mother put her hand on his shoulder. "You must be hungry. Let's eat."

After dinner, Spider sat by the wood stove doing his homework. "Dad, were you ever in a spelling bee?" he asked.

"As a matter of fact, I was."

"Were you scared?"

"I was very scared. I didn't even want do to it. But then my father told me to pretend I was a brave animal, the strongest, bravest animal I could think of. Then I wasn't afraid anymore."

Later, Spider sat up in bed thinking of animals who weren't afraid of anything. Above his head hung the picture of a mountain lion his dad had painted for him. How about a mountain lion, the King of the Beasts?

Spider took his flashlight from under his pillow and shined its beam on the face of the great wild creature. "Brave as a mountain lion," he said to himself in a loud, strong voice.

"Brave as a mountain lion," he repeated in his mind as he was falling asleep.

"I'll try to be brave as a mountain lion," he whispered to his father the next morning as he brushed his hair for school.

At recess the next day Spider peeked into the gymnasium. The huge room was empty. He looked up at the mural painting of the western Shoshone people of long ago. They were brave hunters of deer and antelope and elk, just as his father and his uncles were today.

At the far end of the gym was the scoreboard with the school's emblem, the eagle. Every Saturday in the winter Spider and his whole family came to cheer for Will and the basketball team. Those players weren't afraid of anything.

Then Spider stared up at the stage. That's where the spellers would stand. He could feel his throat tighten and hear his heart thumping, bumpity-bumpity-bumpity-bump. How could he ever get up there in front of all the people? Spider ran outside, slamming the gym door behind him.

That afternoon it was still snowing. At home Spider found his grandmother beading a hatband for his father's birthday. Spider watched her dip her needle into the bowls of red and black and white beads.

"Grandma, were you ever in a spelling bee?"

"No, I never was," his grandmother answered. "Are you thinking much about it?"

"All the time," said Spider.

"What's the worst part?"

"Being up on the stage with all the people looking at you."

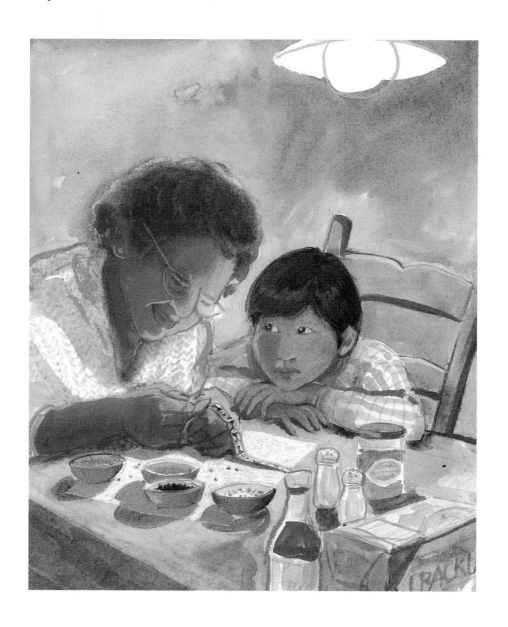

"Oh, that's easy," said his grandmother. "You can be clever. Clever as a coyote. The coyote always has some trick to help him out of trouble. When you're up there on the stage, you don't have to look at the people. You can turn your back on them and pretend they aren't even there."

In bed that night Spider pulled the covers over his head. "Brave as a mountain lion, clever as a coyote," he kept repeating to himself as he fell asleep.

The next morning Spider scraped a peephole in the ice on his bedroom window. He couldn't see the far mountains for the swirling snow. He smiled as he packed his book bag. If it kept snowing like this, maybe the principal would close school tomorrow.

In class that day all everybody could talk about was the spelling bee. "Can we count on you, Spider?" asked Miss Phillips, his teacher.

Spider shook his head. "Maybe," he said. "I haven't made up my mind."

"You'd better make up your mind soon," said Miss Phillips. "The spelling bee is tomorrow night."

After lunch Spider walked by the gym door, but this time he didn't open it. He didn't have to. He remembered just how everything looked. Scary. When he thought about it, a shiver went all the way down his spine.

By the afternoon the snow had piled in drifts higher than Spider's head. Spider got a bowl of popcorn and went to the carport to watch Will shoot baskets. Time after time the ball slipped through the net. Will almost never missed.

"How about some popcorn for me?" Will asked his little brother. Spider brought back another bowl from the kitchen.

"Are you practicing for the spelling bee?" asked Will.

"I've decided not to be in it," said Spider. "I'm going to be brave when I'm bigger."

Will nodded. "I remember those spelling bees."

"Were you afraid?" asked Spider.

"I was scared silly," said Will. "Then I learned the secret."

"What's the secret?" asked Spider.

"To be silent."

"Silent?" asked Spider. "What does that do?"

"It keeps you cool. When I have a hard shot to make and the whole team depends on me, that's when I get very silent."

Spider didn't say anything. He just watched his
brother shooting one basket after another. Then he saw
her. High above the shelves of paint and livestock
medicines was a tiny insect. It was his old friend, Little
Spider, dangling on a long strand as she spun a new
part of her web. She was silent. Silent as the moon.

Spider laughed. How could he have forgotten!
Grandmother often told him how when he was a baby in
his cradle board he used to watch for hours while a little
spider spun her web above his head. She had been his
first friend. Ever since, his family had called him Spider.

Taking the stepladder, Spider climbed up close so
he could watch the tiny creature. How brave she was,
dropping down into space with nothing to hang onto.

And how clever, weaving a web out of nothing but her own secret self. "Say something," he whispered.

The little insect was silent. But Spider felt she was talking to him in her own mysterious way. "Listen to your spirit," she seemed to say. "Listen to your spirit and you'll never be afraid."

———————

The next morning the snow had stopped. Outside Spider's window icicles glistened in the sun. No chance of school being closed today.

"Brave as a mountain lion, clever as a coyote, silent as a spider," Spider thought to himself as he buttoned his vest.

Winona pushed open the door. "Are you going to do it?"

"I'm going to do it," Spider answered.

That night all the family came, his grandmother who lived with them and his other grandparents and his father and his mother and three aunts and two uncles and Will and Winona and lots of their cousins. Three of his cousins were going to be in the spelling bee too.

Brave as a mountain lion, Spider climbed up the steps to the stage. Clever as a coyote, he turned his back so he wouldn't see the rows of people down below. Silently, he listened to his spirit. Bumpity-bump-bump went his heart.

All the best spellers in his class were up there on the stage, standing in a line. The principal gave them the words, one by one.

At first the words were easy. "Yellow," said the principal. "I have a yellow dog."

Spider kept his eyes on the principal's face. "Yellow," said Spider. "Y-e-l-l-o-w. Yellow."

"Correct," said the principal.

Then the words got a little harder. "February," said the principal. "Soon it will be February." It was Spider's turn again.

"February," said Spider, remembering the *r*. "Capital f-e-b-r-u-a-r-y. February."

"Correct," said the principal.

Finally there were only two spellers left standing—
Spider and Elsie, a girl from the other side of the
reservation.

"Terrific," said the principal. "We have a terrific
basketball team."

"Terrific," said Spider, taking a big breath. "T-e-r-r-
i-f-f-i-c. Terrific."

"Incorrect," said the principal. Then she turned
to Elsie. "Terrific. We have a terrific basketball team."

"Terrific," said Elsie, "T-e-r-r-i-f-i-c. Terrific."

"Correct," said the principal. "Let's give a hand
to our two winners from Miss Phillips' class: Elsie
in first place and Spider in second place."

It was over! Spider climbed down the steps and
found the rows where his family was sitting. Spider's
father shook his hand and Will slapped him on the
back. "You did it!" his mother said proudly. "You
stood right up there in front of everybody!"

"It was easy," said Spider.

"You were brave," said his father. "Brave as a mountain lion."

"And clever," said his grandmother. "Clever as a coyote."

I wasn't even afraid, Spider thought. I listened to my spirit. "But now I'm hungry," he told his family. "Hungry as a bear. Let's all go home and eat."

About the Author
Ann Herbert Scott

Ann Herbert Scott has been writing for nearly her whole life. Her parents were proud of her special talent and collected her writings in scrapbooks when she was small.

When Ms. Scott was in her teens and twenties, she worked with inner-city children. At the time, there weren't many books about children like those she worked with. This bothered her. "I dreamed that someday I would write true-to-life stories that would be set in the housing project where I worked," she says. Many years later Ms. Scott wrote *Big Cowboy Western* about a boy who lives in the inner city.

Open for Discussion

Spider has stage fright. If you had to get up on stage in front of your whole school, would you be nervous? Why or why not?

Comprehension Check

1. Think of a movie, video, or TV character who is afraid of something. What would Spider say to that character?

2. Spider changes during the story. Do you think Spider will enter any more contests? Why or why not?

3. List three or four things Spider is advised to be or to do. Which piece of advice would be most helpful to you?

4. Think about the auditorium where the spelling bee takes place. **Visualize** the auditorium and describe it to a friend. What do you see, hear, smell, and feel?

5. Spider and his family are about to celebrate. **Visualize** the celebration. Give details about what they will eat and what they might talk about.

Medal for Bravery

Design a medal for Spider. Remember he was second in the spelling bee but first in bravery to his family.

Spiders

by Avocado Elementary School Teachers and Students

This description of a science experiment comes from a World Wide Web site on the Internet.

Experiment

The spiders in the vivariums were used to conduct an experiment. The students were asked to observe the behavior of the spiders in the vivariums for a week. The vivariums where spiders were kept look like aquariums, but without the water.

Question

Do spiders eat only insects?

Hypothesis

We believe that spiders eat only insects.

Reading Across Texts

Reading an Internet Article

✓ **Read the title.** The title is the topic of the article. If the title is wrong, you may be at the wrong web site. Check the Internet address. Did you type it correctly?

✓ **Look at words in dark or boldface type.** They point out important information.

✓ **Look for words that are underlined or appear in colored type.** They may lead you to more information about your topic.

Focus Your Reading

This Internet article gives information about spiders. As you read, think about how Spider might have used this information.

Avocado Elementary School

Homestead, Florida

Teachers and Staff   Science Inquiry Hotlists   Science Projects

Events   Web Searchers   Technology Projects

Observations

The eating habits of the vivarium spiders were observed for a week on a daily basis. The students paid attention to what the spiders would or would not eat. The students charted their observations on a log. Some of the things that were fed to the spiders are dead bugs, ants, and crickets.

The spiders in our observation were:

- Black widows
- Garden spiders
- Crab spiders
- House spiders
- Banana spiders

We found out that spiders not only eat insects, but they also eat other animals. This includes other spiders, birds, and mice.

Conclusion

What we observed disproves our hypothesis.

What We Learned About Spiders

- Spiders are arachnids.
- Their bodies are in two parts, the head and the abdomen.
- They do not have feelers.
- Most spiders have eight eyes, but some have six, four, or two.
- Many spiders trap their food in webs.
- Not all spiders make webs.
- Some spiders dig homes under the ground.
- Some spiders have claws at the ends of their legs.
- Spiders live in all sorts of environments. Some live under water.

Crab spider

House spider

Black widow

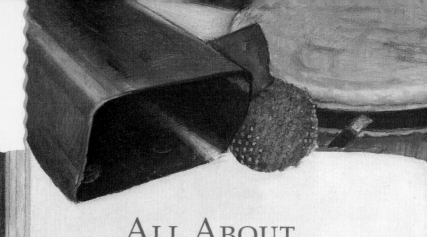

Skill Lesson

Generalizing

- A **generalization** is a statement or rule that applies to many examples.

- You sometimes are given ideas about several things or people. A generalization might say how they are mostly alike or all alike in some way.

- Clue words such as *all, always, everyone, some,* and *never* can signal a generalization.

Read "All About MIMI" from *Mimi's Tutu* by Tynia Thomassie.

Talk About It

1. Look for the clue words *all, always,* and *everyone* in the story. What generalizations does the author make using these words?

2. What generalizations can you make about MIMI's family?

ALL ABOUT
MIMI
by Tynia Thomassie

When MIMI was born, she followed a long line of boys. The family rejoiced at the arrival of their first little girl. Especially the grandmothers.

All the grandfathers and uncles had been honored with namesakes. There was Jacques, for Mama's father, and Emile, after Mama's brother. Clarence and Forest were named for Daddy's father and brother. In fact, there were more boys than uncles and grandfathers to name them after.

Now all the grandmothers and aunts felt that the new baby should be named after *them*. But, there were two grandmothers and two aunts, and only one very small little girl.

That's how she became to be called M'bewe Iecine Magalee Isabella . . . or MIMI for short.

From the time MIMI was a baby, she was always surrounded by music and dance. This was her family's tradition. Grampa Jacques beat out rhythms on the *congas*, while Uncle Forest played the cowbell. Aunt Isabella played the claves and Gramma Iecine shook the brightly beaded *shekere*.

Gramma M'bewe knew the ceremonial dances of Guinea, and Mama was a fine dancer too.

Whenever the family gathered, everyone from the tallest to the smallest grabbed an instrument or danced.

MIMI would bob to the beat or shake her rattle in time to the music.

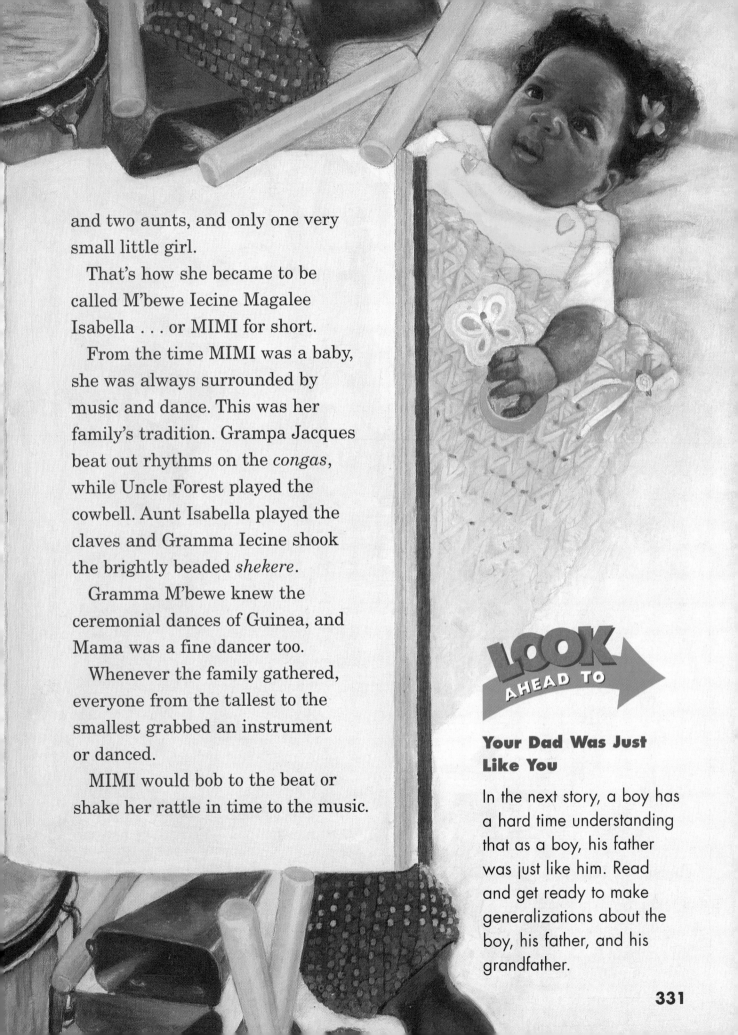

LOOK AHEAD TO

Your Dad Was Just Like You

In the next story, a boy has a hard time understanding that as a boy, his father was just like him. Read and get ready to make generalizations about the boy, his father, and his grandfather.

Words to Know

serious   problem   prove
jokes   neighborhood   prize

Words with similar meanings, like *silent* and *quiet,* are called **synonyms.** You can often figure out the meaning of an unknown word by finding a clue in the words around it. This clue may be a synonym.

Read this paragraph. Notice how *show* helps you understand what *prove* means.

More Alike Than Different

My mom and I are very much alike. We both grew up in the same neighborhood and we both tell jokes when things get too serious. My mother is an award-winning artist, and I won a prize for my painting. We both can solve a math problem easily. Does this show my point? Though sometimes we seem different, these facts prove that we are alike!

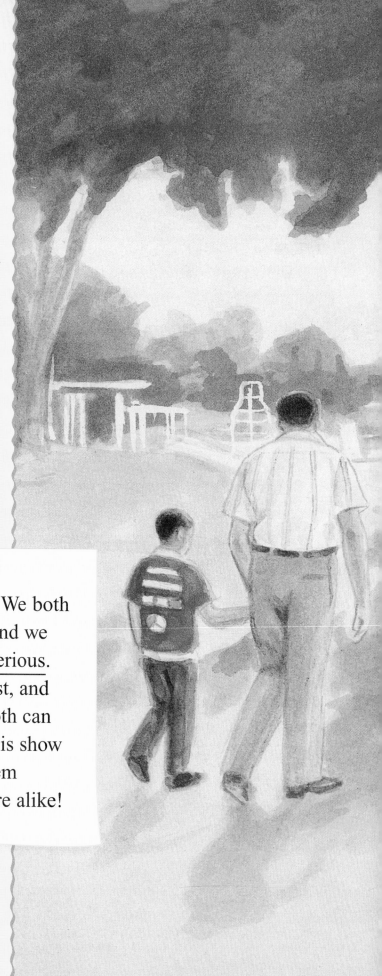

Write About It

Describe how you and a family member or friend are alike and different. Use vocabulary words.

Your Dad
Was Just
Like You

**written and illustrated
by Dolores Johnson**

Peter stood at the front door of his grandfather's house. "You're the best grandpa that ever was," he said. "Can I move in with you?"

"Move in with me? What happened this time? Did you and your dad have another fight?" asked Peter's grandfather. "You two are always battlin'."

"I wasn't doin' anything, Grandpa," said Peter. "I was just playing around—you know—running, and that ole stupid purple thing on Dad's dresser just seemed to jump onto the floor and break. Dad was so mad, he didn't even yell. He was so mad, he just walked away. Grandpa, I think I need to move in with you."

"Why don't we take a walk, Grandson, and sort this problem out? Sometimes my head works better when my legs get a chance to stretch."

The two walked through the neighborhood their family had lived in for years. After they had walked some, Peter sighed, "I wish Dad was more like you, Grandpa. He never smiles—he only yells. 'Look at these awful grades, Peter.' 'You never finish anything you start, Peter.' 'Why can't you be more serious, Peter?' He just never leaves me alone."

"There was a time when your father laughed and smiled all the time," said Peter's grandfather. "When he was a boy, your dad was just like you."

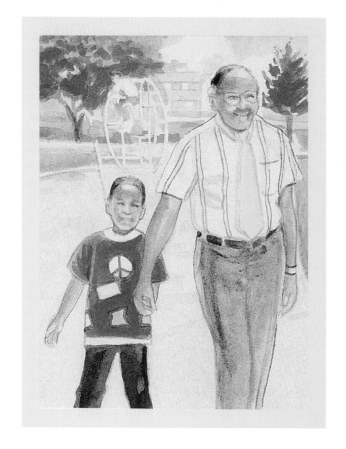

"My daddy was a *boy* . . . just like *me?*" asked Peter.

"That boy would tell me silly jokes just like you tell. When I didn't even feel like smiling, that boy sure could make me laugh. All he had to do was tell his favorite knock knock jokes."

"*My* dad told *knock knock* jokes?" asked Peter. "You sure you're talking about *my* dad?"

"I know it's hard for you to believe," said his grandfather, "but when your father was young, he was like any other boy. Sometimes he played so long at this park, I almost had to drag him home. He played basketball on that court until he almost wore out the net. He even led big game safaris through that jungle gym."

"Dad played in *my* jungle?" asked Peter.

"He played combat with little green army men on the grass by those swings. He practically wore a groove in this sidewalk with his bicycle. But there was one thing that boy loved to do more than anything else in the world."

"What's that, Grandpa?" Peter chuckled. "Yell at the little kids? Start fights?"

"More than living, laughing, or eating, your father loved to run. He ran from sunup to sundown. He ran so fast that his shadow had trouble keeping up with him."

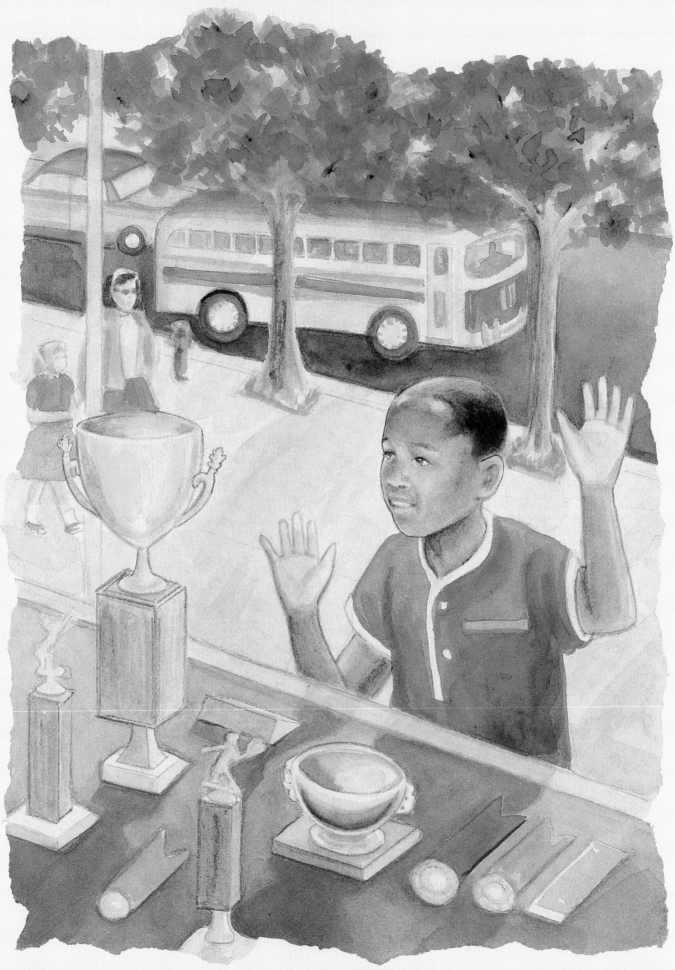

Peter asked, "So why doesn't my dad run now?"

"There came a time when he became serious. And he told himself, a serious man doesn't run."

"Did he ever run in a race?" asked Peter. "Did he ever win a prize?"

"Your father ran only one race, when he wasn't much older than you. It was the biggest race in the town for schoolkids. Your father sure wanted to win that big golden trophy."

"Dad must have lost the race, 'cause I've never seen any big golden trophy. At least not on the bookshelf where he keeps all his special stuff."

"Sometimes you don't compete for trophies just to place them high up on a shelf," said his grandfather. "Sometimes you compete so you can prove something to yourself. When your father was your age, he had something to prove. He was having trouble in school. Nothing seemed to be going right for him."

"But my daddy's so smart!" said Peter.

"He didn't think he was smart, but he *knew* he was fast. He could run like the wind, and he wanted to show everyone. He stopped playing games. He stopped laughing and joking. He ran day and night as fast as he could because he wanted to run that race and win."

"Did he win, Grandpa?"

Peter's grandfather laughed. "Are you going to let me tell my story? Everyone from town—hundreds of people—lined every inch of that one-mile course to the courthouse. About fifty boys and girls gathered at the starting line, fidgeting and milling about like pigeons on a telephone wire. The starter raised his gun. 'On your mark . . . get set . . .' he thundered. And then the worst thing that could possibly happen happened."

"What, Grandpa?"

"A drop of rain fell, and then another and another."

"It started raining?" laughed Peter. "So? I've run a million times in the rain."

"Not rain like this, boy. I looked up, and the sky had turned dark and angry. Rain poured down, and pools of water formed at my feet. The starter didn't have to say 'Go!' because the children had already started running. But they weren't running to the finish line. They were trying to find the last dry spot on earth."

"So Daddy ran for cover too, huh, Grandpa? You know, he doesn't like to mess up his clothes."

"No. It seems your father had something he just had to do. He picked up one leg after the other and ran as fast as he could toward the end of the race.

"And he kept running even though the rain came down so heavy it nearly knocked him down with its force. The wind howled around him, and pools of water were reaching up to drag at his feet."

"Did Daddy ever reach the finish line?"

"Yes, Grandson, but no one was there to congratulate him. No one handed him a big trophy. No one told him how good he was."

"Where were you, Grandpa?"

"I ran behind your father. I didn't catch up to him until the very end. I finally reached him as he stood alone, shaking his head and sobbing in the rain."

"So what did you do, Grandpa?"

"I picked your father up and carried him home. I dried him off and laid him down. And while he probably cried himself to sleep, I sat down with these two big, clumsy hands of mine and made my boy a trophy, because he really deserved one."

"So where is the trophy now, Grandpa?"

"Well, it . . . it was . . ." said the old man.

"Was it a big ole stupid purple . . . ? Oh, I'm sorry, Grandpa. What did Dad say when you gave it to him?"

"He didn't really say much at all . . . just, 'I love you, Dad,' for the very first time. You see, when your father was a boy, he and I used to fight a lot.

I used to yell at him. I hardly ever smiled. We decided to change what was wrong between us. That day, we became a real serious father and son."

"I've got to go home now, Grandpa. There's something serious I've got to do," said Peter. He hugged his grandfather tightly, and then ran the short distance home.

When Peter got home, he gathered the purple pieces that still lay in a heap in his father's bedroom. Then the boy brought them to his own bedroom and worked very hard to make what was broken whole again.

Peter stood in the doorway of the living room and watched his father read in silence. Then the little boy said just three words, even though he was so nervous he felt like running away. "Knock, knock, Dad."

His father hesitated for just a moment, looked up, smiled, and said, "Who's there?"

About the Author/Illustrator
Dolores Johnson

Dolores Johnson was an artist and didn't know it. "When I was young," she says, "I knew I could draw, but I didn't think I was an artist." She knew her brother was an artist, because he was always drawing or painting. But she liked things besides art too.

So when they grew up, Ms. Johnson's brother got a job as an artist. She herself tried many different jobs but kept working on art projects at night. One day a friend saw some of her paintings and writings. She told Ms. Johnson that she should create a children's book. Five years later, her illustrations were published in her first book. Now she writes the words for many of her books too.

Ms. Johnson remembers how things felt when she was a child and writes about those feelings. She writes about how it feels to go to a baby-sitter, to come home to an empty house, or to have trouble getting along with someone you love.

Now Ms. Johnson knows that she is an artist, and she loves being one. She feels a great responsibility to the children who read her books. "I hope that they might find as much pleasure reading my books as I have writing them," she says.

Reader Response

Open for Discussion

What happens when someone breaks something that belongs to someone else? How do the people feel? What should each one do?

Comprehension Check

1. In what ways are Peter and his dad alike?

2. Spider in *Brave as a Mountain Lion* comes in second in the spelling bee, and Dad as a boy doesn't even get to race. Compare how the two boys must have felt.

3. What do you think will happen after Peter gives the mended trophy to Dad?

4. Think about both Spider and Dad. Make a **generalization** about how important a contest can be.

5. Think about what the story tells about how Peter and Dad get along, and also how about Dad and Grandpa got along. What can you **generalize** about how some fathers and sons get along?

Act It Out

Imagine Peter, Dad, and Grandpa talking about the trophy Peter mended. What would each one say and do? With two classmates, act out what you think would happen.

The Steam Shovel

by Rowena Bennett

The steam digger
Is much bigger
Than the biggest beast I know.
He snorts and roars
Like the dinosaurs
That lived long years ago.

He crouches low
On his tractor paws
And scoops the dirt up
With his jaws;
Then swings his long
Stiff neck around
And spits it out
Upon the ground

Oh, the steam digger . . .
Is much bigger
Than the biggest beast I know.
He snorts and roars
Like the dinosaurs
That lived long years ago.

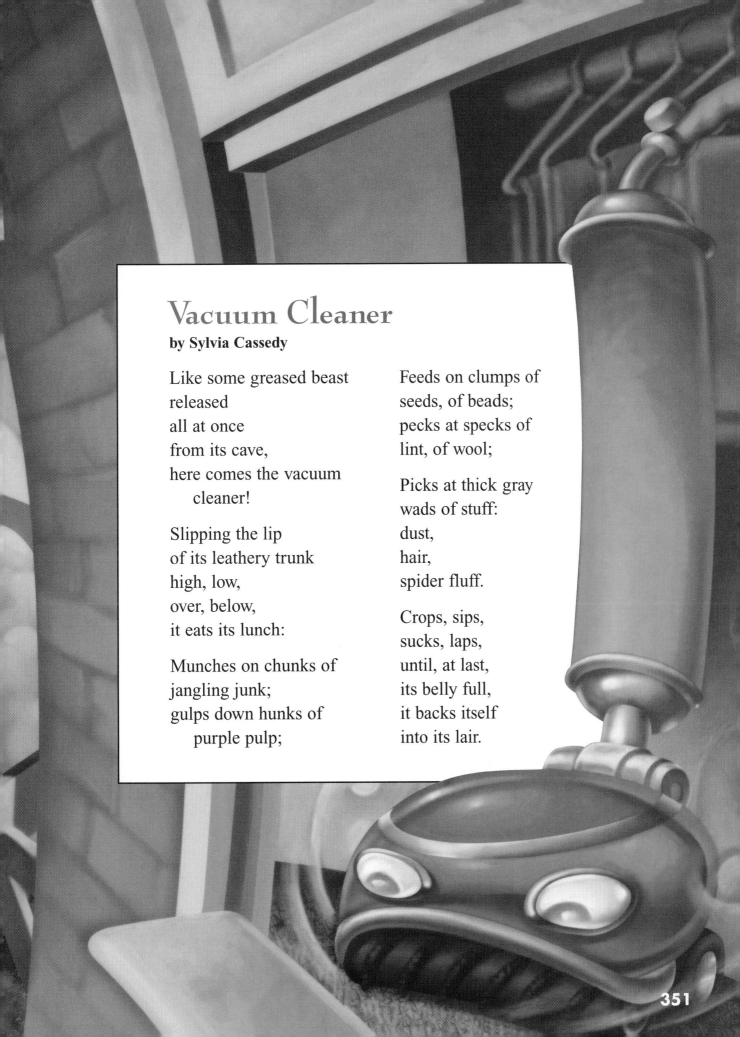

Vacuum Cleaner

by Sylvia Cassedy

Like some greased beast
released
all at once
from its cave,
here comes the vacuum
    cleaner!

Slipping the lip
of its leathery trunk
high, low,
over, below,
it eats its lunch:

Munches on chunks of
jangling junk;
gulps down hunks of
    purple pulp;

Feeds on clumps of
seeds, of beads;
pecks at specks of
lint, of wool;

Picks at thick gray
wads of stuff:
dust,
hair,
spider fluff.

Crops, sips,
sucks, laps,
until, at last,
its belly full,
it backs itself
into its lair.

Lineage

by Margaret Walker

My grandmothers were strong.
They followed plows and bent to toil.
They moved through fields sowing seed.
They touched earth and grain grew.
They were full of sturdiness and singing.
My grandmothers were strong.

My grandmothers are full of memories.
Smelling of soap and onions and wet clay
With veins rolling roughly over quick hands
They have many clean words to say.
My grandmothers were strong.
Why am I not as they?

Honor

by Alma Flor Ada

Honor is the work
we do in the fields.
Honor is a family
who loves and cares for one another.
Honor is being true to myself
as I wake up each morning.

Honor

por Alma Flor Ada

Honor es el trabajo
que hacemos en los campos.
Honor es la familia
que se quiere y se apoya.
Honor es ser quien soy,
al despertar cada mañana.

Glossary

How to Use This Glossary

This glossary can help you understand and pronounce some of the words in this book. The entries in this glossary are in alphabetical order. There are guide words at the top of each page to show you the first and last words on the page. A pronunciation key is at the bottom of every other page. Remember, if you can't find the word you are looking for, ask for help or check a dictionary.

The entry word is in dark type. It shows how the word is spelled and how the word is divided into syllables.

The pronunciation is in parentheses. It also shows which syllables are stressed.

Part-of-speech labels show the function or functions of an entry word and any listed form of that word.

ap•ply (ə plī′), VERB. to put on: *Apply another coat of paint after the first one has dried.* ❑ VERB **ap•plies, ap•plied, ap•ply•ing.**

Sometimes, irregular and other forms will be shown to help you use the word correctly.

The definition and example sentence show you what the word means and how it is used.

354

A a

a•fraid (ə frād′), ADJECTIVE. frightened; feeling fear: *She was afraid of fire.*

aim (ām), VERB. to point or direct something at a goal or target: *She aimed the arrow at the target.* ❑ VERB **aims, aimed, aim•ing.**

a•lert (ə lėrt′), ADJECTIVE. watchful; wide-awake: *The dog was alert to every sound.*

ap•ply (ə plī′), VERB. to put on: *Apply another coat of paint after the first one has dried.* ❑ VERB **ap•plies, ap•plied, ap•ply•ing.**

au•thor (ȯ′thər), NOUN. someone who writes books, poems, stories, or articles; writer: *She is one of my favorite authors.*

author

B b

bas·ket·ball (bas′kit bȯl′), NOUN.
1 a game played with a large, round ball between two teams of five players each. The players score points by tossing the ball through baskets hanging at either end of the court.
2 the ball used in this game.

bounce (bouns), VERB
1 to spring into the air like a ball: *The baby likes to bounce up and down on the bed.*
2 to cause to bounce: *She bounced the ball to me.*
❑ VERB **bounc·es, bounced, bounc·ing.**

bound¹ (bound), VERB. to leap or spring lightly along; jump: *The mountain goat bounded from rock to rock.* ❑ VERB **bounds, bound·ed, bound·ing.**

bound² (bound), VERB. to form the boundary of; limit: *The United States is bounded by Canada on the north.* ❑ VERB **bounds, bound·ed, bound·ing.**

brave (brāv), ADJECTIVE. without fear; showing courage: *The brave woman went into the burning house to save a baby.* ❑ ADJECTIVE **brav·er, brav·est.**

break (brāk),
1 VERB. to come apart or make come apart: *This cheap toy breaks easily.*
2 NOUN. a broken place; crack: *There was a break in the wall. The X ray showed a break in my leg.*
❑ VERB **breaks, broke, bro·ken, break·ing.**

break·fast (brek′fəst), NOUN. the first meal of the day.

breathe (brēᴛʜ), VERB. to draw air into the lungs and force it out. You breathe through your nose or through your mouth. ❑ VERB **breathes, breathed, breath·ing.**

bur·ro (bėr′ō), NOUN. a donkey used to carry loads or packs in the southwestern United States and Mexico. ❑ PLURAL **bur·ros.** ■ Another word that sounds like this is **burrow.**

a	hat	ė	term	ô	order	ch	child		
ā	age	i	it	oi	oil	ng	long	a in about	
ä	far	ī	ice	ou	out	sh	she	e in taken	
â	care	o	hot	u	cup	th	thin	ə	i in pencil
e	let	ō	open	ů	put	ᴛʜ	then	o in lemon	
ē	equal	ȯ	saw	ü	rule	zh	measure	u in circus	

bur•row (bėr′ō), NOUN. a hole dug in the ground by an animal for shelter or protection. Rabbits live in burrows. ▪ Another word that sounds like this is **burro.**

busi•ness (biz′nis), NOUN. work done to earn a living; occupation: *A carpenter's business is building things.* ❑ PLURAL **busi•ness•es.**

C c

card•board (kärd′bôrd′), NOUN. a stiff material made of layers of paper pulp pressed together, used to make cards, boxes, and so on.

car•toon•ist (kär tü′nist), NOUN. someone who draws cartoons.

cheat (chēt), VERB. to deceive or trick someone; do business or play in a way that is not honest: *I refused to play the game with her because she cheated.* ❑ VERB **cheats, cheat•ed, cheat•ing. –cheat′er,** NOUN.

clev•er (klev′ər), ADJECTIVE. bright; intelligent; having a quick mind: *She is the cleverest person in our class.*

cliff (klif), NOUN. a very steep, rocky slope.

col•lect (kə lekt′), VERB. to bring things together; gather together: *Our teacher will collect our homework this morning.* ❑ VERB **col•lects, col•lect•ed, col•lect•ing.**

com•fort•a•ble (kum′fər tə bəl), ADJECTIVE. giving comfort: *A soft, warm bed is comfortable.*

comfortable

con·cen·trate (kon′sən trāt), *VERB.* to pay close attention: *I will concentrate on my reading so that I understand the story.* ❏ *VERB* **con·cen·trates, con·cen·trat·ed, con·cen·trat·ing.**

con·fi·dent (kon′fə dənt), *ADJECTIVE.* firmly believing; certain; sure: *I feel confident that our team will win.*

con·ser·va·tion·ist (kon′sər vā′shə nist), *NOUN.* someone who wants to preserve and protect the forests, rivers, and other natural resources of a country: *Conservationists stopped them from cutting down the trees.*

cor·rect (kə rekt′), *VERB.* to change something to a better condition or to agree with some standard: *Your manners need some correcting.* ❏ *VERB* **cor·rects, cor·rect·ed, cor·rect·ing.**

cough (kȯf), *VERB.* to force air out of your throat with a loud noise: *He coughs when there is dust in the air.* ❏ *VERB* **coughs, coughed, cough·ing.**

cow·boy (kou′boi′), *NOUN.* a man who works on a cattle ranch or at rodeos: *Several cowboys worked on our ranch.*

co·zy (kō′zē), *ADJECTIVE.* warm and comfortable; snug: *The cat lay in a cozy corner near the fireplace.* ❏ *ADJECTIVE* **co·zi·er, co·zi·est.**

cur·i·ous (kyu̇r′ē əs), *ADJECTIVE.* eager to know: *Small children are very curious, and they ask many questions.*

D d

de·stroy (di stroi′), *VERB.* to damage something very badly; ruin or smash: *A tornado can destroy a house.* ❏ *VERB* **de·stroys, de·stroyed, de·stroy·ing.**

destroy

a	hat	ė	term	ô	order	ch	child	⎧a in about
ā	age	i	it	oi	oil	ng	long	⎪e in taken
ä	far	ī	ice	ou	out	sh	she	ə⎨i in pencil
â	care	o	hot	u	cup	th	thin	⎪o in lemon
e	let	ō	open	u̇	put	ŦH	then	⎩u in circus
ē	equal	ȯ	saw	ü	rule	zh	measure	

dif·fi·cult (dif′ə kult), ADJECTIVE.
1 hard to do or understand: *Math is difficult for some students.*
2 hard to deal with or get along with; not easy to please: *My cousin is difficult and is always unhappy.*

di·rec·tion (də rek′shən), NOUN. any way in which you may face, point, or go: *Please point me in the direction of the cafeteria.*

dis·cov·er (dis kuv′ər), VERB. to find out something that was not known before: *Scientists have discovered a new type of medicine.* ❏ VERB **dis·cov·ers, dis·cov·ered, dis·cov·er·ing.**

dream (drēm), NOUN.
1 thoughts, feelings, and mental images during sleep: *I had a bad dream last night.*
2 something like a dream; daydream; wish: *I have dreams of becoming a famous scientist.*

E e

eas·i·ly (ē′zə lē), ADVERB. without trying hard; with little effort: *The simple tasks were easily done.*

ex·per·i·ence (ek spir′ē əns), NOUN. things that are seen, done, or lived through: *We had several pleasant experiences on our trip. People learn by experience.*

ex·per·i·ment (ek sper′ə mənt), NOUN. a carefully planned trial or test to find out something: *We made an experiment to learn the weight of the air in a basketball.*

eye (ī), NOUN.
1 the part of the body that people and animals use for seeing.
2 the calm, clear area at the center of a hurricane.

F f

fa·vor·ite (fā′vər it), ADJECTIVE. liked better than others: *What is your favorite flower? My favorite sports are soccer and softball.*

fo·rest (fôr′ist), NOUN. a large area with many tall trees; thick woods: *Many animals live in the forest.*

Gg

gift (gift), *NOUN.* something given; present: *I saved my allowance to buy my sister a birthday gift.*

gob·ble¹ (gob′əl), *VERB.* to eat very quickly: *The children gobbled their candy.* ❑ *VERB* **gob·bles, gob·bled, gob·bling.**

gob·ble² (gob′əl),
1 *NOUN.* the noise a turkey makes.
2 *VERB.* to make this noise or one like it. ❑ *VERB* **gob·bles, gob·bled, gob·bling.**

grand·fa·ther (grand′fä′ᴛʜər), *NOUN.* the father of your father or mother.

guide (gīd), *NOUN.* someone or something that shows the way: *The guide led us on a trail through the woods.*
❑ *PLURAL* **guides.**

Hh

har·ness (här′nis), *NOUN.* the leather straps, bands, and other pieces used to hitch a horse or other animal to a carriage, wagon, or plow. ❑ *PLURAL* **har·ness·es.**

har·vest (här′vist), *VERB.* to gather crops: *We are harvesting the corn this month.* ❑ *VERB* **har·vests, har·vest·ed, har·vest·ing.**

hatch (hach), *VERB.* to come out of an egg: *The chicks should hatch today.*
❑ *VERB* **hatch·es, hatched, hatch·ing.**

hatch

a	hat	ė	term	ô	order	ch	child		a in about
ā	age	i	it	oi	oil	ng	long		e in taken
ä	far	ī	ice	ou	out	sh	she	ə	i in pencil
â	care	o	hot	u	cup	th	thin		o in lemon
e	let	ō	open	ủ	put	ᴛʜ	then		u in circus
ē	equal	ò	saw	ü	rule	zh	measure		

hinge (hinj), NOUN. a joint on which a door, gate, cover, or lid moves back and forth so that it can open and close.

hun·gry (hung′grē), ADJECTIVE. feeling a need to eat: *I missed breakfast and was hungry all morning.* ❏ ADJECTIVE **hun·gri·er, hun·gri·est.**

hur·ri·cane (hėr′ə kān), NOUN. a fierce storm with very strong, dangerous winds and, usually, very heavy rain. The wind in a hurricane blows at more than 75 miles per hour.

hy·poth·e·sis (hī poth′ə sis), NOUN. something assumed to be true because it seems likely; theory: *Before the experiment, we formed a hypothesis of what we expected to observe.* ❏ PLURAL **hy·poth·e·ses** (hī poth′ə sēz′).

Ii

i·mag·i·na·tion (i maj′ə nā′shən), NOUN. the power to make pictures or ideas in the mind of things not present to the senses. A poet, artist, or inventor must have imagination to create new things or ideas or to combine old ones in new forms.

in·for·ma·tion (in′fər mā′shən), NOUN. knowledge given or received of some fact or event; news: *An encyclopedia contains much information.*

in·sect (in′sekt), NOUN. any of a group of very small animals without bones, with bodies divided into three parts. Insects have three pairs of legs and one or two pairs of wings. Flies, mosquitoes, butterflies, beetles, and bees are insects.

insects

in·tro·duce (in′trə düs′), VERB. to tell people each other's names when they don't know each other: *I will introduce my new friend to my family.* ❏ VERB **in·tro·duc·es, in·tro·duced, in·tro·duc·ing.**

is·land (ī′lənd), *NOUN.* a body of land surrounded by water: *Hawaii is made up of a group of islands.*

Jj

joke (jōk), *NOUN.* a short, funny story you tell to make people laugh: *He told several jokes at the party.*

Ll

la·zy (lā′zē), *ADJECTIVE.* not willing to work or move fast: *He lost his job because he was lazy.* ❑ *ADJECTIVE* **la·zi·er, la·zi·est.**

li·brar·y (lī′brer′ē), *NOUN.* a room or building where a collection of books, magazines, films, or recordings is kept for public use and borrowing: *We checked three libraries before we found the book.* ❑ *PLURAL* **li·brar·ies.**

Mm

melt (melt), *VERB.* to turn something from a solid into a liquid by heating it. Ice becomes water when it melts. ❑ *VERB* **melts, melt·ed, melt·ing.**

mu·se·um (myü zē′əm), *NOUN.* a building for displaying a collection of objects illustrating science, ancient life, art, or other subjects: *We visited two museums to see their new displays.*

Nn

neigh·bor·hood (nā′bər hůd), *NOUN.* people living near one another: *The whole neighborhood came to the big party.*

news·pa·per (nüz′pā′pər), *NOUN.* sheets of paper printed every day or week, telling the news, carrying advertisements, pictures, articles, and useful information.

noise (noiz), *NOUN.* an unpleasant or disturbing sound: *The noise kept me awake all night.*

Oo

ob·ser·va·tion (ob′zər vā′shən), *NOUN.* something seen and noted: *During science experiments she kept careful records of her observations.*

a	hat	ė	term	ô	order	ch	child		a in about
ā	age	i	it	oi	oil	ng	long		e in taken
ä	far	ī	ice	ou	out	sh	she	ə {	i in pencil
â	care	o	hot	u	cup	th	thin		o in lemon
e	let	ō	open	ů	put	ᴛʜ	then		u in circus
ē	equal	ò	saw	ü	rule	zh	measure		

o•cean (ō′shən), *NOUN.* the great body of salt water that covers almost three fourths of the Earth's surface; the sea.

Pp

part•ner (pärt′nər), *NOUN.* a member of a company who shares the risks and profits of the business: *Three business partners bought my mother's old company.*

paste (pāst), *VERB.* to stick things together with glue: *Paste the orange paper onto the black paper.* ❑ *VERB* **pastes, past•ed, past•ing.**

pa•tient (pā′shənt), *ADJECTIVE.* able to wait quietly for something that you want: *We need to be patient while we are standing in line.*

pitch•er (pich′ər), *NOUN.* a container with a lip at one side and a handle at the other. Pitchers are used for holding and pouring out liquids.

plan•et (plan′it), *NOUN.* one of the nine large astronomical objects that move around the sun. Mercury, Venus, Earth, Mars, Jupiter, Saturn, Uranus, Neptune, and Pluto are planets.

plant (plant), *NOUN.* any living thing that can make its own food from sunlight, air, and water. Plants cannot move about by themselves. Trees, bushes, vines, grass, vegetables, and seaweed are all plants.

play•ground (plā′ground′), *NOUN.* a place to play outdoors.

po•em (pō′əm), *NOUN.* a piece of writing that expresses the writer's imagination. In poems, the patterns made by the sounds of the words have special importance.

pow•er•ful (pou′ər fəl), *ADJECTIVE.* having great power or force; strong: *The principal is a powerful person. My illness improved after the doctor gave me some powerful medicine.*

planet

prac·tice (prak′tis), NOUN. an action done many times over to gain skill: *Practice makes perfect.*

pre·pare (pri pâr′), VERB. to get something ready; to get yourself ready for doing something: *We all helped prepare a picnic lunch. When the bell rings, we all prepare to go outside.* ❑ VERB **pre·pares, pre·pared, pre·par·ing.**

pre·tend (pri tend′), VERB. to make believe something, just for fun: *Let's pretend that we are grown-ups.* ❑ VERB **pre·tends, pre·tend·ed, pre·tend·ing.**

prize (prīz), NOUN. something you win for doing something well; reward: *Prizes will be given for the best stories.*

prob·lem (prob′ləm), NOUN. a question or situation, especially a difficult one: *Poverty is a national problem.*

prom·ise (prom′is), VERB. to say or write that you will do or will not do something: *I promise to come to your party.* ❑ VERB **prom·is·es, prom·ised, prom·is·ing.**

prove (prüv), VERB. to show that something is true: *Prove your statement.* ❑ VERB **proves, proved, proved** or **prov·en, prov·ing.**

Rr

ref·uge (ref′yüj), NOUN. shelter or protection from danger or trouble.

res·er·va·tion (rez′ər vā′shən), NOUN. land set aside by the government for a special purpose: *My aunt is a doctor on an Indian reservation.*

ro·de·o (rō′dē ō *or* rō dā′ō), NOUN. a contest or show in which cowboys and cowgirls show their skills. They ride wild horses, steers, and bulls, and rope cattle. ❑ PLURAL **ro·de·os.**

Ss

scar·y (skâr′ē), ADJECTIVE. making someone feel afraid: *We watched a scary movie.* ❑ ADJECTIVE **scar·i·er, scar·i·est.** –**scar′i·ness,** NOUN.

a	hat	ė	term	ô	order	ch	child		a in about
ā	age	i	it	oi	oil	ng	long		e in taken
ä	far	ī	ice	ou	out	sh	she	ə	i in pencil
â	care	o	hot	u	cup	th	thin		o in lemon
e	let	ō	open	ů	put	ŦH	then		u in circus
ē	equal	ò	saw	ü	rule	zh	measure		

363

search (sėrch), VERB. to look through; go over carefully; examine, especially for something hidden: *The police are searching the prisoners to see if they have weapons.* ❑ VERB **search•es, searched, search•ing.**

se•cret (sē′krit), ADJECTIVE. kept from the knowledge of others: *The army had a secret plan to win the war.*

ser•i•ous (sir′ē əs), ADJECTIVE. thoughtful; not humorous: *We had a serious discussion about classroom safety.*

sheet (shēt), NOUN.
1 a large piece of cloth, usually of linen or cotton, used on a bed to sleep on or under.
2 a single piece of paper.

shoot (shüt), VERB. to send a ball, puck, or the like toward the goal while scoring or trying to score: *We went to the gym to shoot baskets.* ❑ VERB **shoots, shot, shoot•ing.** **–shoot′er,** NOUN.

shoot

si•lent (sī′lənt), ADJECTIVE. without any noise; quiet; still: *She tiptoed through the silent house late at night.*

space (spās), NOUN. the unlimited room or emptiness that exists in all directions: *The Earth moves through space.*

space•ship (spās′ship′), NOUN. a vehicle used for flight in outer space; spacecraft.

Span•iard (span′yərd), NOUN. someone born or living in Spain: *Two Spaniards came to visit us in the United States.*

Span•ish (span′ish), ADJECTIVE. of or about Spain, its people, or their language.

spell•ing (spel′ing), NOUN. the act or skill of writing or saying the letters of a word in order: *I need to work on my spelling.*

storm (stôrm), NOUN. a strong wind, usually with heavy rain, snow, or hail. Some storms have thunder and lightning.

sug·ges·tion (səg jes′chən *or* sə jes′chən), *NOUN.* something proposed as an idea: *The songs were excellent suggestions.*

sum·mer (sum′ər), *NOUN.* the warmest season of the year, between spring and autumn.

Tt

tech·nique (tek nēk′), *NOUN.* a special method or system used to do something. ❑ *PLURAL* **tech·niques.**

thou·sand (thou′znd), *NOUN OR ADJECTIVE.* ten hundred; 1,000: *There were thousands of people at the concert.*

tor·na·do (tôr nā′dō), *NOUN.* a very violent and destructive windstorm with winds as high as 300 miles per hour; twister. A tornado extends down from a mass of dark clouds as a twisting funnel and moves across the land in a narrow path. ❑ *PLURAL* **tor·na·does** or **tor·na·dos.**

tour·ist (tùr′ist), *NOUN.* someone traveling for pleasure: *Each year many tourists go to Canada.*

trace (trās), *VERB.* to copy by following the lines of something with a pencil or pen: *Put thin paper over the map and trace it.* ❑ *VERB* **trac·es, traced, trac·ing.**

trap (trap), *NOUN.* a device for catching animals: *The mouse was caught in a trap.*

trou·ble (trub′əl), *NOUN.* something that upsets, bothers, or worries you, or that gives you pain: *The trouble began when our car broke down in a storm.*

tornado

a	hat	ė	term	ô	order	ch	child		a in about
ā	age	i	it	oi	oil	ng	long		e in taken
ä	far	ī	ice	ou	out	sh	she	ə	i in pencil
â	care	o	hot	u	cup	th	thin		o in lemon
e	let	ō	open	ù	put	ŦH	then		u in circus
ē	equal	ò	saw	ü	rule	zh	measure		

U u

un·der·ground (un′dər ground′), ADVERB. beneath the surface of the ground: *Most miners work underground.*

United States (yü nī′tid stāts), a country in North America, extending from the Atlantic to the Pacific and from the Gulf of Mexico to Canada. Alaska, the 49th state, lies northwest of Canada. Hawaii, the 50th state, is a group of islands in the Pacific.

V v

va·ca·tion (vā kā′shən), NOUN. a time when you are not at school or at work: *Our family took a long vacation last year.*

vis·it (viz′it), VERB. to go to see someone and spend some time there: *I visit my friend every week.* ❑ VERB **vis·its, vis·it·ed, vis·it·ing.**

W w

warn·ing (wôr′ning), NOUN. something that warns; notice given in advance: *We were given many warnings about the bad weather.*

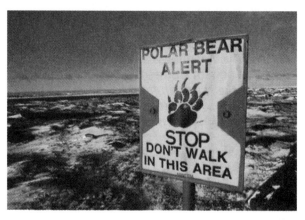

warning

wealth (welth), NOUN. a large quantity; riches: *The king shared his great wealth with the kingdom.*

west (west), NOUN. the direction of the sunset.

whooping crane (hüp′ing krān or wüp′ing krān), a large white crane having a loud, hoarse cry. Whooping cranes are now almost extinct.

wrecked (rekt), ADJECTIVE. completely destroyed or ruined: *The storm left a trail of wrecked homes, cars, and trees.*

a	hat	ė	term	ô	order	ch	child		a in about
ā	age	i	it	oi	oil	ng	long		e in taken
ä	far	ī	ice	ou	out	sh	she	ə	i in pencil
â	care	o	hot	u	cup	th	thin		o in lemon
e	let	ō	open	ù	put	ŦH	then		u in circus
ē	equal	ò	saw	ü	rule	zh	measure		

Acknowledgments

Text

Page 14: From *Arnie Goes to Camp* by Nancy Carlson. Copyright © 1988 by Nancy Carlson. Reprinted by permission of Viking Kestrel, a division of Penguin Putnam, Inc.

Page 16: *How I Spent My Summer Vacation* by Mark Teague. Copyright © 1995 by Mark Teague. Reprinted by arrangement with Crown Publishers, Inc.

Page 39: Excerpt from *Pecos Bill* by Ariane Dewey. Text copyright © 1983 by Ariane Dewey. Reprinted by permission of Greenwillow Books, a division of William Morrow & Company, Inc.

Page 44: From *Three up a Tree* by James Marshall. Copyright © 1986 by James Marshall. Reprinted by permission of Dial Books for Young Readers, a division of Penguin Putnam, Inc.

Page 46: *Goldilocks and the Three Bears* by James Marshall. Copyright © 1988 by James Marshall. Reprinted by permission of Dial Books for Young Readers, a division of Penguin Putnam, Inc.

Page 70: "A Cowboy's Rope" from *The Cowboy's Handbook* by Tod Cody. Copyright © 1996 by Breslich & Foss. Reprinted by permission of Cobblehill Books, an affiliate of Dutton Children's Books, a division of Penguin Putnam, Inc.

Page 72: Text from *Anthony Reynoso: Born to Rope* by Martha Cooper and Ginger Gordon. Text copyright © 1996 by Ginger Gordon. All rights reserved. Reprinted by permission of Clarion Books/Houghton Mifflin Company.

Page 89: Adapted excerpt from *Kids Explore America's Hispanic Heritage.* Copyright © 1996, 1994 by Jefferson County School District No. R-1. Published by John Muir Publications, Santa Fe, New Mexico. Reprinted by permission.

Page 90: From *Herbie Jones* by Suzy Kline. Copyright © 1985 by Suzy Kline. Reprinted by permission of G. P. Putnam's Sons, a division of Penguin Putnam, Inc.

Page 92: From *Herbie Jones Reader's Theater* by Suzy Kline. Text copyright © 1992 by Suzy Kline. Reprinted by permission of G. P. Putnam's Sons, a division of Penguin Putnam, Inc.

Page 108: From *Because You're Lucky* by Irene Smalls. Illustrated by Michael Hays. Text copyright © 1997 by Irene Smalls. Illustrations copyright © 1997 by Michael Hays. Reprinted by permission of Little, Brown and Company.

Page 110: *Allie's Basketball Dream* by Barbara E. Barber. Illustrated by Darryl Ligasan. Text copyright © 1996 by Barbara E. Barber. Illustrations copyright © 1996 by Darryl Ligasan. Reprinted by permission of Lee & Low Books Inc.

Page 129: Reprinted courtesy of *Sports Illustrated for Kids* from the January 1998 issue. Copyright © 1998, Time, Inc. "SWISH!" by Andrea N. Whittaker. All rights reserved.

Page 132: "My Brother Is as Generous as Anyone Could Be" from *Something Big Has Been Here* by Jack Prelutsky. Text copyright © 1990 by Jack Prelutsky. Reprinted by permission of William Morrow & Company.

Page 133: "Summer Vacation" from *My Daddy Is a Cool Dude and Other Poems* by Karama Fufuka. Text copyright © 1975 by Karama Fufuka. Reprinted by permission of Dial Books for Young Readers, a division of Penguin Putnam, Inc.

Page 134: "Poem" from *Collected Poems by* Langston Hughes. Copyright © 1994 by the Estate of Langston Hughes. Reprinted by permission of Alfred A. Knopf, Inc.

Page 134: "Watering/Regar" from *Gathering the Sun* by Alma Flor Ada. English translation by Rosa Zubizarreta. Text copyright © 1997 by Alma Flor Ada. Reprinted by permission of Lothrop, Lee & Shepard Books, a division of William Morrow & Company, Inc.

Page 135: "August afternoon" from *Open the Door* by Marion Edey and Dorothy Grider. Text copyright 1949 Marion Edey and Dorothy Grider. Reprinted by permission of Atheneum Books for Young Readers, an imprint of Simon & Schuster Children's Publishing Division. (NY, Charles Scribner's Sons, 1949)

Page 138: From *What's Inside of Plants* by Herbert S. Zim. New York: William Morrow & Company, Inc. 1952, pp. 4–5.

Page 140: *Fly Traps! Plants That Bite Back* by Martin Jenkins. Copyright © 1996 by Martin Jenkins. Published by Candlewick Press, Cambridge, MA. Reprinted by permission of Walker Books Limited, London.

Page 159: Adapted from "Can You Catch Flies?" by Rhonda Lucas Donald. Illustration by Tan Branch Graphics. Text copyright © 1996 by the National Wildlife Federation. Illustration copyright © 1996 by Tan Branch Graphics. Text reprinted from the April 1996 issue of *Ranger Rick Magazine* with the permission of the publisher, the National Wildlife Federation.

Page 162: From *The Willow Umbrella* by Christine Widman. Text copyright © 1993 Christine Widman. Reprinted with the permission of Simon & Schuster Books for Young Readers, an imprint of Simon & Schuster Children's Publishing Division.

Page 163: From *Roger's Umbrella* by Daniel M. Pinkwater. Illustrated by James Marshall. Copyright © 1982 by Daniel M. Pinkwater. Reprinted by permission of Dutton, a division of Penguin Putnam, Inc.

Page 164: *Guys from Space* by Daniel Pinkwater. Copyright © 1989 by Daniel Pinkwater. Reprinted by permission of Atheneum Books for Young Readers, Simon & Schuster Children's Publishing Division.

Page 180: From *Weather* by Martha Ryan. Reprinted by permission of Grolier Publishing Company.

Page 182: *Tornado Alert* by Franklyn M. Branley. Text copyright © 1988 by Franklyn M. Branley. Reprinted by permission of HarperCollins Publishers.

Page 198: From "My Favorite Sharks" by Don Reed from *Boys Life* Magazine, June 1993. Reprinted by permission of Don C. Reed.

Page 200: *Danger—Icebergs!* by Roma Gans. Text copyright © 1987 by Roma Gans. Reprinted by permission of HarperCollins Publishers.

Page 214: From *Discovering Sea Birds* by Anthony Wharton. Artwork by Wendy Meadway. First published in 1987 by Wayland Publishers. Reprinted by permission of Wayland Publishers Ltd., East Sussex, England.

Page 216: *Nights of the Pufflings* by Bruce McMillan. Text copyright © 1995 by Bruce McMillan. All rights reserved. Reprinted by permission of Houghton Mifflin Company.

Page 232: From *Peeping in the Shell* by Faith McNulty. Illustrations by Irene Brady. Text copyright © 1986 by Faith McNulty. Illustrations copyright © 1986 by Irene Brady. Reprinted by permission.

Page 236: "Clouds" from *In the Woods, in the Meadow, in the Sky* by Aileen Fisher. Copyright © 1965 by Aileen Fisher. Copyright renewed 1993 by Aileen Fisher. Reprinted by permission of Marian Reiner for the author.

Page 238: "Laughing Tomatoes" from *Laughing Tomatoes* by Francisco X. Alarcón, 1997. Text copyright © 1997 by Francisco X. Alarcón. All rights reserved. Reprinted by permission of Children's Book Press.

Page 239: "Fishes' Evening Song" from *Whispering and Other Things* published by Alfred A. Knopf. Copyright © 1967 by Dahlov Ipcar. Reprinted by permission of McIntosh and Otis, Inc.

Page 242: From *Cartooning for Kids* by Carol Lea Benjamin. Copyright © 1982 by Carol Lea Benjamin. Reprinted by permission of the author.

Page 244: From *What Do Authors Do?* by Eileen Christelow. Text and illustrations copyright © 1995 by Eileen Christelow. All rights reserved. Reprinted by permission of Clarion Books/Houghton Mifflin Company.

Page 266: Excerpt from "A Perfect Gift" in *The Blue Hill Meadows* by Cynthia Rylant. Copyright © 1997 by Cynthia Rylant. Reprinted by permission of Harcourt Brace & Company.

Page 268: *Tops and Bottoms* by Janet Stevens. Copyright © 1995 by Janet Stevens. Reprinted by permission of Harcourt Brace & Company.

Page 290: From *Puppy Training and Critters, Too!* by Judy Peterson-Fleming and Bill Fleming. Reprinted by permission of Tambourine Books, a division of William Morrow & Company, Inc.

Page 292: Excerpt from *Mom's Best Friend* by Sally Alexander. Text copyright © 1992 by Sally Alexander. All rights reserved. Reprinted by permission of the author and Book Stop Literary Agency.

Page 306: From *A Net of Stars* by Jennifer Richard Jacobson. Copyright © 1998 by Jennifer Richard Jacobson. Reprinted by permission of Dial Books for Young Readers, a division of Penguin Putnam, Inc.

Page 308: *Brave as a Mountain Lion* by Ann Herbert Scott. Text copyright © 1996 by Ann Herbert Scott. Illustrations copyright © 1996 by Glo Coalson. All rights reserved. Reprinted by permission of Clarion Books/Houghton Mifflin Co.

Page 328: "Spiders" Experiment from *Avocado Elementary School Website* by Carmen Johnson and Carol Ann Delancy, Avocado Elementary School, Homestead, Florida. Reprinted by permission.

Page 330: From *Mimi's Tutu* by Tynia Thomassie. Copyright © 1996 by Tynia Thomassie. Reprinted by permission of Scholastic, Inc.

Page 332: *Your Dad Was Just Like You* by Dolores Johnson. Copyright © 1993 by Dolores Johnson. Reprinted by permission of Atheneum Books for Young Readers, Simon & Schuster Children's Publishing Division.

Page 350: "The Steam Shovel" from *Story-Teller Poems* by Rowena Bennett. Copyright 1948 by Rowena Bennett. Reprinted by permission of K. C. Bennett.

Page: 351: "Vacuum Cleaner" from *Zoomrimes: Poems About Things That Go* by Sylvia Cassedy. Copyright © 1993 by Sylvia Cassedy. Reprinted by permission of HarperCollins Publishers.

Page 352: "Lineage" from *This Is My Century: New and Collected Poems* by Margaret Walker Alexander. Text copyright © 1989 by Margaret Walker Alexander. Reprinted by permission of the University of Georgia Press.

Page 353: "Honor/Honor" from *Gathering the Sun* by Alma Flor Ada. English translation by Rosa Zubizarreta. Text copyright © 1997 by Alma Flor Ada. Reprinted by permission of Lothrop, Lee & Shepard Books, a division of William Morrow & Company, Inc.

Artists

Cover: Daniel Craig
Pages 14–15: Harry Roolaart
Pages 16–38: Mark Teague
Pages 39–43: JoAnn Adinolfi
Pages 44–45, 46-69: James Marshall
Pages 70–71: Jeff Meyer
Page 89: John Sandford
Pages 90–91, 92–105: Don Stewart
Pages 110–128: Darryl Ligasan
Pages 132–135: Larry Johnson
Pages 138–139: Marty Blake
Pages 140–158: David Parkins
Pages 162–163: Franklin Hammond
Pages 164–177: Daniel Pinkwater
Pages 180–181, 182–197: Joel Spector
Pages 198–199: Larry Day
Pages 203–205, 207, 209–211: Ebet Dudley
Pages 214–215 (Inset): Wendy Meadway
Pages 232–235: Irene Brady
Pages 236–239: Lee Lee Brazeal
Pages 240–241: Mike Reed
Pages 242–243 (Inset): Carol Lea Benjamin
Pages 244–264: Eileen Christelow
Pages 266–267: Susan Leopold
Pages 268–289: Janet Stevens

Pages 290–291: Don Stewart
Pages 306–307: Joel Spector
Pages 308–326: Glo Coalson
Pages 328–329 (Web Art): Tony Klassen
Pages 330–331: Gabriela Dellosso
Pages 332–347: Dolores Johnson
Pages 350–353: Darryl Ligason

Photographs

Page 11: Sharon Hoogstraten
Pages 12–13: Ed Honowitz/Tony Stone Images
Page 37: Richard Hutchings for Scott Foresman
Page 68: Courtesy Houghton Mifflin Co.
Pages 73–86: Martha Cooper
Page 87: (T) Martha Cooper; (B) Jim Norman
Page 106: Courtesy Suzy Kline, Photographer: Dalla Valle (Inset)
Pages 106–107, 108–109: Sharon Hoogstraten
Page 127: Richard Hutchings for Scott Foresman
Pages 129–130: Manny Millan/Sports Illustrated
Page 131: (B) Manny Millan/Sports Illustrated; (BKGRD) Nathaniel S. Butler/NBA/Sports Illustrated; (T-INSET) Manny Millan/Sports Illustrated
Pages 136–137: T. Davis/W. Bilenduke/Tony Stone Images
Page 159: John Netherton
Page 178: Kathy McLaughlin
Page 180: (INSET) NASA
Page 183: Superstock
Page 185: Beryl Bidwell/Tony Stone Images
Page 188: Charles Doswell/Tony Stone Images
Page 190: (B) Spencer Tirey/Liaison Network; (TL, TR) AP/Wide World
Page 191: David J. Sams/Tony Stone Images
Page 192: NASA
Pages 200–201: Price/OSF/Animals Animals
Page 202: David Muench/Tony Stone Images
Page 206: Corbis/UPI/Bettmann
Pages 208–209: John Beatty/Tony Stone Images
Page 212: Special Collections, Milbank Memorial Library, Teachers College, Columbia University
Pages 214–215: © IFA/West Stock
Pages 216–231: Bruce McMillan
Page 230: (B) Benner McGee
Pages 242–243: Sharon Hoogstraten (Backgrounds)
Page 265: (ALL) ©1996 Sean Higgins
Pages 287–288: Courtesy Janet Stevens
Pages 292–303: George Ancona
Page 304: (T) Courtesy Sally Hobart Alexander; (B) Courtesy George Ancona
Page 326: Lawrence Migdale for Scott Foresman
Page 329: (T) Richard Shiell/Animals Animals/Earth Scenes; (C) Bruce MacDonald/Animals Animals/Earth Scenes; (B) Joe MacDonald/Bruce Coleman Inc.
Page 348: Courtesy Dolores Johnson

Glossary

The contents of the glossary have been adapted from *Beginning Dictionary*, copyright © 1999, Scott Foresman and Company.